Lone Survivor at Shiloh

By

Duane Helweg

Copyright © 2008 Duane Helweg

No part of this book may be reproduced or utilized in any form or by any means: electronic, mechanical or otherwise, including photocopying, recording or by any informational storage and retrieval system without permission in writing from the author.

Although the author has researched all sources to ensure the accuracy and completeness of the information contained within this book, no responsibility is assumed for errors, inaccuracies, omissions, or inconsistency herein. Any slights of people, places or organizations are completely and totally unintentional.

ISBN
1-933177-14-4 (10 digit)
978-1-933177-14-4 (13 digit)

Library of Congress Control Number: 2009921113

Second Edition 2011

Cover photo and design by the author; depicting the field grain, fescue, as "cane." The words "all is well, safely rest" are from the military "Taps," played at days end.

Published by Lone Star Productions
13820 Methuen Green, Dallas, TX 75240
(972) 671-0002

Available From:
Rimrock Writings
4370 Rimrock Circle, San Angelo TX 76904
(325) 245-8628
Web site: www.RimrockWritings.com
Email: info@rimrockwritings.com

Dedication

I dedicate this to my great grandmother, born *Mary Lucrecia Wicker*, who without her sharing of Shiloh, this work would not be, and to my late mother, born *Wanda Louise Montgomery*, who not only helped take care of Mary in her last years, but also saw me through polio and a tornado at age six. There's nothing as healing as a mother's love. Her cup was always half-full, not half-empty, and so she taught me. Such is my inheritance.

Acknowledgements

My first word of thanks must go to a now former ranger at Shiloh National Military Park, Dr. Timothy B. Smith, for being aware of and providing me a copy of the 1934 research paper whose history content named my 3rd great grandfather, 'Louis' Wicker, as the builder of the cabin at the park. Without such, this work would never be.

Obviously, another to whom I owe a debt of gratitude is Chief Park Ranger Stacy Allen. He provided battle days' military input and editing, plus copies of data in park files. Also thanks go to Park Ranger Thomas Parson for providing me copies of historical and personal pictures of the cabin to scan, plus, a copy of his preservation project report.

Another obvious person to thank is my wife, Sharon, for her support. Also, Ginnie Bivona & Lone Star Productions.

After the above, a myriad of people deserve a word of thanks for their contributions, no matter how large or small. I shall try to enumerate all:

Members of my Wicker family, in no particular order, are:

Hurshell Tillman
Lisa Wicker
Mildred Blount
Bobbye Strickland
Linda Wicker
Cindy Mclaughlin
Howard Montgomery
Anease Meier
Nina (Wicker) Anderson
Cliff Wicker

Shiloh, TN or area locals:

Wallace Fullwood
Dr. Ronnie Fullwood
Sallie (Reaves) White
Larry DeBerry
Miriam (Bell) Holden
David Cagle
Connie Lewis, Savannah Library
Hardin County Register of Deeds:
 Julie Adkisson, Register of Deeds
 Nancy Lumpkin

Others:

Joanne Baucum
Jo Anna (George)
Barbara Foster
Vicki Betts, Reference Librarian
Joe Weiss
Dr. Brian McKnight
Dr. Ellen Shlasko
San Angelo Writer's Club
 Ross McSwain, Travis Monday
West Texas Collection
 Suzanne Campbell
David Burk

Table of Contents

Prologue:
This Is My Greatest Journey

This is my greatest journey. It is not that I survived, first, polio at age six, thereby losing the use of an arm, then later that same year to survive the loss of my home from a tornado, with me in it. It is not that I finished college, found a spiritual life, got married and raised two children, found success at playing tennis and in a job.

My greatest journey is in this book. It is a piece of me. It is a piece of those who came before me. It fills a niche in a place and in a time that no one else has filled. With books abounding all around, telling the story and stories of Shiloh, whirring about in the mind, covering what one would think, saying what one would say, all about an infamy unique in American history, one would think that no more could be said…but not so.

Lying quietly in the middle of a great battlefield is a simple log cabin. It is just a wooden structure that once housed family, or families in it. It is, however, a survivor. There it survived storm of shell and storm of nature. Perhaps crying out from its walls are the voices of all those who cried from the loss of their homes, who cried about the loss of possessions and who cried the most over the loss of life…family or otherwise.

In the now mostly fallow fields around it, many such losses occurred. The mandate by man there today is the military story. Mine is the poignant story of people…the people who lived here, the ones who lived in cabins like the one that survives. It cries out to say, "We were here, too. We suffered losses too; of flesh and fodder, of blood and bed, of mind and matter, of breath and beauty."

This is my greatest journey, to tell the story of a simple cabin, simple families, and simple lives, complicated only by the closeness of the call of causes. Now envision the entry of invasion, the need to flee from fear, the sanctity of survival. While written words of wisdom have filled the hallowed highway of history here, the cabin has lay silent for most of that time. Now it speaks and I give it a voice. It is my unction, it is my honor.

This is my greatest journey…listen to the words of those who had no voice here, listen to the words of those who did, listen to the words of your heart and be still…all is well…safely rest within the cradle of the cabin. It still speaks, and in speaking for it…this…has been my greatest journey.

Duane Helweg

Introduction

We have a saying here in Texas where I grew up. When one sees an old vacated farm or ranch house that lies in ruin or a state of disrepair you say, "If only walls could talk, the stories they would tell…" Such would truly be the case of the lone dwelling structure to survive the Civil War Battle of Shiloh, remaining within the battleground proper.

The old log "War Cabin," as originally called, has a history to tell, more than surviving the battle itself, and I want to tell it. If you visit Shiloh National Military Park in Tennessee, where the cabin is located, it will be identified as the "Manse George Cabin." He and his family are definitely part of its history, but only part of it. Although not displayed in park history, my Wicker family not only built the cabin, and later re-owned it after Mr. George, but my family was even more involved in its full history timeline.

I was intrigued as a youngster in Texas hearing my mother recount her grandmother, Mary Lucrecia (Wicker) Strawn/Montgomery, telling about the sights and sounds of Shiloh. My mother helped care for Mary in her final years. My own children were college educated in Tennessee, and upon coming to visit them I naturally stopped at the park. I made inquiry of the name "Wicker" at the Visitor Center. The ranger on duty pointed out a "Wicker Field" on their main map, talked of a "Widow Wicker" and of a potential feud that developed around the turn of the last century between the Wickers and Joneses.

It wasn't until a later visit that I had the good fortune to encounter a young park ranger, Dr. Timothy B. Smith, who was writing a book on the park administrative history, *This Great Battlefield of Shiloh.*[1] He had become aware of two things in his effort that would influence my desire to do research myself and write this work. One was a research paper contained in the park files, finished in April of 1934 by a member of the Civil Works Administration at Shiloh, Tennessee, during the Great Depression.

It was designed to show how the old cabin was built and how to restore it. Contained therein is some of its history, including that Lewis Wicker (spelled "Louis" in the paper) built the structure. He was identified as the builder through an interview of his grandson, John W. Wicker, who himself owned the land and cabin, after Mr. George, from 1885 to 1896. This was the second piece of data shared by Ranger Smith, in the form of an ownership map from mid-1890. Thereafter, I volunteered to do deed research in Savannah, Tennessee for him in the battle era period, and, the 1890's, when at that time the War Department began buying lands for the park, established by Congress in 1894.

In doing research at the park and on my Wicker family there, the history of the cabin becomes more than the battle itself, or the move of the cabin, and, its eventual sale to the USA as part of the park. This is the history of the cabin as I know it, before, during and after the battle that left it scarred with bullet holes, perhaps evident even today. I will share some of what the cabin "experienced" and potentially endured over the years, from its creation by 1849, through its park restoration, preservation, and rehabilitation in 2003.

I have researched deeds, tax lists, military records, censuses, books, family histories, the Internet and interviewed in producing this work. From being "raised" by 1849, to its

[1] Timothy B. Smith, *This Great Battlefield of Shiloh: History, Memory, and the Establishment of a Civil War National Military Park* (Knoxville: The University of Tennessee Press, 2004).

latest "facelift" by the park in 2003, the old cabin, if it could talk, would have a story, or stories, to tell. I have endeavored to tell them for it, in delivering this history to the reader. Although factual as best I know, any deductions or speculations made by me are at least fact-based, whether written or oral family histories, and possible to have occurred.

Cabins are about people, and to write a cabins history without telling how they lived, about their daily lives, what they did, what they ate, would be a short and dull telling of a history. Memoirs and a diary help overcome that. Although these writers never specifically ever lived in the old cabin in question, how they lived could not be that much different. I ask the reader to forgive some personal family inclusions in this historical work, as it is not my intent to make this a family history. However, upon investigation and analysis, the Wickers were either directly involved as owners, or as neighbors to this cabin, even after its move, for over half of its 150-plus year history. No other family comes close to matching that. Whether it's by fate or by fortune, the Wicker's were a big part of the cabins history, and thus it reads. I have tried to weave a family thread therein.

The family names "George" and "Wicker" are tied together on several occasions in this work. This includes, the Wickers being from, and William George possibly being from, Lincoln County, to the eventual move of some of the Wickers next door to Mr. George. Becoming neighbors may have led to a connection to, or at least an awareness of, a vacant cabin, built by the Wickers and perhaps maintained in ownership (as my research suggests), residing on Perry Field where Mr. George obtained it after the battle to move. Then there is a re-ownership in 1885 of the cabin by the Wickers, in whatever state or for whatever purpose, up until at least the sale of that land to the USA. Then based on census data, they remained occupants there or certainly at the very least neighbors, until 1930 and maybe as long as 1934, and even beyond. Therefore, it is difficult to separate the Wickers family history and influence, from the cabins history, and must be addressed.

A cabin was the "hub" of a wheel of life in those days, and life radiated out from it like the spokes of a true wagon wheel…also of that day.

When you read the contents of this work that has been put together, reflected upon and compiled, think in terms of the influence on the cabin itself, its occupants or others of the day, or in the eras covered. That way you as a reader will see and feel and get to know, the fullness of the cabins history, both directly and indirectly. It has "experienced" much over its lifetime. One just has to see it within this framework.

Chapter 1: Lone Survivor at Shiloh

It laid witness to one of the bloodiest encounters of the Civil War...Shiloh...and survived, being the only dwelling structure remaining in the park today that was within the battleground proper, albeit on the fringe on battle days. This is a history from its perspective; the little log cabin that remains in Shiloh National Military Park, Tennessee, known there originally as the "War Cabin," today as the "Manse George Cabin." It is much more, however, than the name of the person who bought and moved it after the battle from near today's park entrance, to its present site among battle names, "Peach Orchard," the "Bloody Pond," and along the famous Sunken Road, or "Hornet's Nest."

According to a research paper (contained in park files) written by Miss Lear Durbin, Assistant Historian of the Civil Works Administration at the park in 1934, the cabin itself was originally built by "Louis" Wicker. Research indicates it was built, or "raised" as they said in those days, by at least 1849. In order to understand where and why it was built, we must look at a bit of the Wicker family history.

In about 1824 in Chatham County, North Carolina, Lewis Wicker married Flora Buchanan.[2] What brought Lewis and family to Tennessee remains unknown to this writer. As we will see later, it was not bounty land given for his service in

[2] Richard Fenton Wicker, Jr., ed., *The New Whicker/Wicker Family, Rev. and Enl.* (Virginia Beach, VA: Wicker Publishing, 1997), 160.

either the military or some war. Perhaps it was just that great westward quest for more "elbow room" that we have all learned about in the annals of our American history.

The Wicker's came to Tennessee by 1830, as Lewis Wicker is in the Lincoln County census. He is also in the 1840 census there and all the ages and genders (which are all that is recorded in that census) match his family. Tax records available for Lincoln reveal that Lewis "W." Wicker is still there in 1846 through 1848 tax times, but not 1849-1850.

The Tennessee State Library says taxes were levied within 30 days of May 1st each year.

We then know that Lewis and family had moved to Hardin County on the west side of the Tennessee River sometime after that 1848 tax listing. Per the October of 1850 census, ten out of eleven of Lewis and Flora's children had come with them, as second son, Alvis (possible future cabin occupant), remained in Lincoln County, working for a farmer.

However, that left six grown or teenage sons, plus a grown daughter and three other girls under age ten, to help build a cabin, or, certainly make need for one. That number of bodies to house and bed down would undoubtedly influence the cabin design. Another event that dates the cabin was the August of 1849 marriage of oldest son Joseph Calvin Wicker to Barbra Catherine Hagy. Her family had been on the river there since 1825.[3]

On the frontier of Hardin County, in speaking about the history of development there, the following is stated:

While most of these early settlements were on the east side of the river, a survey of land titles reveals that the area now within the boundaries of Shiloh National Military Park was first settled around 1828, although the bulk of settlement

[3] "Catfish Hotel - History," The Catfish Hotel, http://catfishhotel.com/history.htm.

occurred in the period 1843 to 1851.[4]

Lewis was either the first purchase owner or an assignee of the 400 acres he eventually sold as first recorded transactions in Hardin County deeds. Following are two e-mails received from the Tennessee State Library and Archives in answer to a query as to Lewis Wicker having any grants:

The index to Tennessee Land Grants does not list a grant, neither a North Carolina nor a general grant, for Lewis Wicker…Most land grants in Tennessee were purchased grants and were, in fact, first ownership of the land. After that all land transactions should show up in the county records.

Lewis was not found at the library records with a purchase grant. Therefore he could have been an assignee, as the following 2nd e-mail indicates:

An assignee is the individual who obtains the land, not necessarily the person who has an entry for the land. Sometimes the individual who has an entry has no desire for the land but holds it for a period so the price will go up…Lewis Wicker could very likely be the assignee…

Future personal research at the Tennessee State Library and Archives uncovered that he was, indeed, an "assignee" of the land. Sometimes as a writer, personal connections you make over time in doing research, uncovers the unconnected. Such is the case in finding the microfilmed land records for Lewis Wicker. In purchasing books about Shiloh on a previous trip there, one had been bought called, *Shiloh's House of*

---

[4] Charles E. Shedd, Jr., Park Historian, "A History of Shiloh National Military Park Tennessee, 'The Coming of the White Man,'" *Park Administration and History, Shiloh National Military Park*, http://www.nps.gov/archive/shil/admhisint3.htm.

Peace, The Church That Named the Battle, by Dr. Ronnie Fullwood. In it he indicated his grandmother lived in the cabin in 1905.[5] Naturally he was contacted for more information and that led to an invitation for this author to speak to the Shiloh Sons of Confederate Veterans Camp.

In doing so, connections with people at that meeting would become instrumental in this history. The first is Larry DeBerry, who does Shiloh tours, and provided family histories of neighbors to the cabin at its present location. Then a Wicker family member at the meeting, Hurshell Tillman (ancestors spelled it 'Tilghman'), the next day provided a letter written in 1999, from the park, in response to an inquiry about his ancestor's park lands. It stated that the "G. W. Tilghman tract is part of the original Lewis Wicker Land Grant (November 24, 1847)…Entry No. 1723, in the name of Lewis Wicker…" Thus this author was off to Nashville seeking details unfound in the two above responses from the Tennessee State Library and Archives.

There, found in Entry Number 1723 on microfilm roll 50 of the Hardin County Tennessee Survey Books, Volume 5, covering years 1842 to 1853, was the following:

State of Tennessee Hardin County; Lewis Wicker assignee of Joseph Crownover & Austin Hatty Entry 400 acres of land in accordance with an act of the General Assembly of Said State passed the 2nd of November 1847 on the waters of Snake Creek in Range 6 & Section 2 & 3 Beginning on the Southwest Corner of Entry No 1829 in the name of Joseph Crownover, Thence East 207 poles, Thence North 88 poles, Thence East 12 poles, North 236 poles, West 136 poles, South 42 poles, West 83 poles, South 252 poles to the beginning – 6 November 1848

Lewis Wicker [Recorder's initials 'SC' entered]

[5] Dr. Ronnie Fullwood, *Shiloh's House of Peace, The Church That Named the Battle* (Selmer, TN; G & P Printing Services, 2003), 10.

(See Appendix #1 for a copy of the original entry)

In order to clarify for the reader, the term "poles" is the measurement data used for that era and location. Other terms are "chains" and "rods," or, in the authors Southwest deed experience, the Spanish term "vara" was utilized in deeds or land descriptions. Our counterparts for today would be feet and yards, or the metric system measures. Poles are the same measurement distance as rods, 16.5 feet in a pole or rod.

The "Wicker boys" would have to be careful deciding which trees to cut to build the cabin with because of how land ownership was marked, as stated in deeds. In measuring poles, when a distance was reached whereby a direction change was needed, they in essence "picked" the closest tree where possible as a "marker." In the land west of the Tennessee River this was quite doable with the density of forest. They then called out the particular tree type (oak, pine etc.). Then, to avoid future confusion, should the marker tree die, fall or be somehow removed, they also scored adjacent trees known as "pointers." These trees carried cuts, like arrows, pointing to the marker tree.[6] All trees were called out as such on deeds, as were any entries, surveys and in some, ownerships.

Evidently the cabin was built by late 1848, as possession of the land occurred at the November 6th entry date and Lewis had to be in Hardin County for the transaction to be entered in the survey books. Since they were gone from Lincoln County by the 1849 tax roll listing, it is doubtful he would have left his family there, over 100 miles to the east, and then moved them with the hard of winter coming. Perhaps well before Christmas, Lewis and Flora Wicker's six grown or near grown sons could be seen felling oak, pine or poplar trees for the cabin and clearing land, as one older daughter and four younger ones helped, along with a female slave. Christmas of

[6] David Cagle, Cagle Engineering, interview by author, Savannah, TN, 2003.

1848 would be a "cabined" one.

What were the other forest building materials found by the "Wicker boys" to use? What wild game and birds did they hunt, or what fish to catch to eat? Answers are as follows:

The forest of Hardin has a greater variety, and perhaps more valuable timber, than any county in the State. There are as many as six species of oak, viz., the white oak, red oak, black oak, willow oak, chestnut oak, and post oak...The hickory is very plentiful...The cypress is used very extensively for well-curbing and shingles...This forest furnishes the county with plenty of timber for pine lumber. The other varieties are the cedar, the chestnut, elm, persimmon, sugar and other maples, poplar, sassafras, black walnut, birch, beech, and ash.

In the first days of civilization, this part of the State was well stocked with wild animals...deer...bear...panther, wild cat, and wolf...the gray and red fox, raccoon, opossum, muskrat, rabbit, squirrel, mink, otter, and beaver...The latter lives in the river bottom, where he builds his house of wood and mortar across the large ponds or old river bed...The wild turkey - the hunter's choice bird - is found in some parts of the county...

The river and creeks in Hardin abound in fine fish, such as the catfish, trout, perch, pike, eel, and buffalo. No county in the State, except Lake, is so plentifully supplied with fish as Hardin. The principal way of procuring them is by means of traps in the creeks and trot-lines and nets in the river.[7]

When the Wickers came to this bountiful part of the country, it appears from records in the upcoming 1850 census that they may have brought a 24 year-old female house slave

[7] B. G. Brazelton, *A History of Hardin County, Tennessee* (Nashville, TN: Cumberland Presbyterian Publishing House, 1885), Chapter XIV (unnumbered), at TNGENWEB, Gene Hosey, transcriber, http://www.geocities.com/Heartland/Meadows/6273/hardin/braz_title.html.

with them. The term "house slave" is used because the Wickers brought "built-in" field hands with them from Lincoln County…seven of the first eight Wicker offspring, being grown or near grown sons, could do that work for the family.

Their slave apparently had, at that time, three small children; a six year old female and a two year-old female, plus an infant son. The 1850 census did not ask for a record of a slave quarters like the 1860 one. However, it is likely that one was built, either attached to the main cabin, or connected by an open, roofed area (a *dog-trot*).[8] Meals probably would have been prepared and eaten in the slave portion with the main cabin used only for sleeping the Wickers.

Again, based on future records with ages shown, the mother and the oldest slave daughter may have remained with the Wickers through the next census (1860), when a slave quarters was recorded as existing in their new family location, next to where the old cabin would be moved to in another two years, 1862. Upon being eventually freed, one wonders where the slaves went and what became of them?

How Was The Cabin Built?

Before answering that question, the following is a little history of the log cabin here in America and then some building ideas. It is from a National Park Service interactive web site, where it says (with this author's inserts):

Determining the Facts
Reading 1: The Log Cabin Tradition

…The Scots, Irish, and Scots-Irish [many of them Tennessee settlers] had no tradition of building with logs, but

[8] Melody Key, "The Pioneer Log Cabin: Productive Resources in Arkansas," *Bessie B. Moore Center for Economic Education*, http://bmcee.uark.edu/default.asp?target=teachingresources&show=lessons.

they quickly adopted the technique. The log cabin suited early settlers and later pioneers... It would have been...difficult to transport building materials on horseback or even in the wagons or river barges pioneers used to cross mountains and valleys in their search for their own land. So, wherever there were forested areas, the log cabin became the preferred type of initial dwelling. Log cabins did not even need nails or spikes to hold them together. Until the 19th century nails were made by hand by blacksmiths, which meant they were quite expensive, and like lumber, they were also heavy.

Log cabins were relatively easy to build. Weslager reports that a record was set by three men who cut down trees, trimmed them, dragged the logs to the building site, notched the logs, and built a one-room cabin with chimney and fireplace in two days. For most people it took a bit longer, but it was possible for a man working alone to build a cabin in one to two weeks. However, a man alone faced some problems. Because it is physically difficult to lift a heavy log above one's head, most men could build cabins only six to eight logs high. With help, it was possible to build several logs higher...First, skids of two logs were placed against the wall at an angle to serve as an inclined plane. Then forked sticks or ropes were used to position the logs.

Most log cabins had a single room, or "pen," some 12 to 16 feet square. There was one door, and usually no windows. If windows were cut into the walls, animal skins or boards fixed to slide across the openings were used. Some builders used paper greased with animal fat, which made it both translucent and waterproof. Most log cabin builders placed the fireplace at one end of the cabin and built the chimney of wattle [a fabrication of poles interwoven with slender branches, withes, or reeds and used especially formerly in building[9]]. Stone or clay was used for the hearth and the interior of the fireplace.

[9] *Dictionary and Thesaurus - Merriam-Webster Online*, http://www.merriam-webster.com.

As these were not very safe constructions, later builders used brick or stone if they could be obtained. Fireplaces provided warmth, light, and fuel for cooking.

Back bars and cranes made of forged iron were used to hold cooking pots. Not until the 1840s were cast-iron ranges available that would burn wood or coal, so cooking over a fireplace did not seem a hardship.

Inside walls were often chinked with clay or cloth. Most floors were simply beaten earth, although some cabins had floors of puncheons–logs split lengthwise and laid close together with the flat sides up. A family often built a sleeping loft if the roof were high enough. The loft could be reached by pegs pounded into the walls or by a ladder built from tree limbs. [It] also was used to store foodstuffs.

<u>Log cabins were never meant to be permanent</u>, but many log houses were. The difference between the two was primarily one of size and attention to detail. Most pioneers preferred "flat" walls to rounded log walls, and so most used hewn logs for building. These not only made the houses look (from a distance) more "real," but also withstood the elements much better, since the bark and the decay-prone outside wood were removed from the logs.

A…factor that kept the tradition of log building alive was the Great Depression of the 1930s. The Civilian Conservation Corps (CCC) worked with the National Park Service and the U.S. Forest Service to build thousands of log structures throughout the national forests and parks. [10]

Now returning to the Wicker cabin; the best record of

[10] C. A. Weslager, *The Log Cabin in America: From Pioneer Days to the Present* (New Brunswick, N.J.: Rutgers University Press, 1969); Virginia and Lee McAlester, *A Field Guide to American Houses* (New York: Alfred A. Knopf, 1984); at NPS: visitor's guides to several western national parks; and other sources on the history of the western frontier, http://www.nps.gov/nr/twhp/wwwlps/lessons/4logcabins/4facts1.htm.

its original means of construction is from Miss Durbin's 1934 research paper (including further detail in her draft copy), plus another paper of hers on chimney's, all of whose intent was to show how cabins were built in the mid-1800's era and to be able to restore and preserve the cabin. Following is an excerpt from the original paper which actually describes it in 1934 and not the late 1840's, but we can easily assume it was originally built close to this manner:

...the house comprises one large hewed log room with a second story. The floor is of tongued and grooved plank. Rough plank and riven boards cover the cracks between the logs. The ceiling overhead forms the floor of the upstairs room. It is laid of rough plank on sawed joists. The stairway that leads to this floor is located in a corner of the room on the left of the fireplace. Its base is only a short distance from the wall, and the staircase makes an unbroken line toward the chimney to the ceiling. Riven boards cover the roof. This upstairs room is not ceiled, and the rafters and lathing are exposed to view. The chimney was made of stick-and-dirt...and the fireplace is closed with plank...A warping board was made on one of the walls by inserting wooden sticks in the holes which were arranged for the purpose. Shelves were also made by laying a plank on two sticks which were placed in holes that were bored by an augur [sic – 'auger'] a short distance from each other. The doors of this house were made of rough plank. There is one in both the north and the south side of the house. [11]

(See Appendix #2 for definition of some of the above terms)

---

[11] Lear Durbin, Assistant Historian, Civil Works Administration, Shiloh National Military Park, TN, "The 'War Cabin'– It's History and Proposed Construction" (Research paper, SNMP, April, 1934).

Further details of chimney building can be seen in another paper written by Miss Durbin in 1934. It states the importance to the community of the chimney builder. Lewis Wicker may well have brought that knowledge with him from his twenty years experience in Lincoln County. However, if so, he probably would still have had to make local inquiry as to the location of a clay pit of which Lear Durbin speaks below:

STICK-AND-DIRT CHIMNEY

Before the time of bricks, concrete, and various other kinds of building materials now popularly used for building, people were forced to resort to the use of materials that were workable and near at hand. In few instances in early architecture, are there shown greater skill and ingenuity than in the making of the stick-and-dirt chimney that almost always adorned the gable ends of the crude but not always simple log cabins.

The chimney builder was a man of vast importance in the community where he, by the use of his head and hands, raised the structure that conveyed the smoke away from the fire that warmed the family and cooked its food. After the "house raising" wherein every one that was able to lift one end of a log did his part in helping his neighbor, the chimney builder was sent for and he completed the home.

About the first thing he did upon his arrival was to locate a pit where clay of the proper kind might be obtained. Only the very finest of clay was to be used, for a chimney was expected to last several years and if properly constructed would endure for twenty years or more. A pure red clay without sand or other foreign matter was the only kind that would stick and hold fast in all kinds of weather, so it was considered luck to find a pit near at hand that was workable.

All the soil was cleared off until nothing but clay remained, then into this was poured water until the mud worked to the proper consistency. Often salt was put into it to make it hard when it dried. Into this mud, rolls of grass, about two feet long and about one to two inches in diameter, were dipped until thoroughly saturated. These rolls were usually pulled and prepared by the lesser members of the family.

The grass kept the mud together and made it easier to put on the frame. These rolls were laid with about two-thirds of its length on the outside of the sticks that formed the frame and the other portion on the inside to protect the sticks from fire. After all this was finished water would be poured on and with trowels or hands the rolls would be slicked down flat, cementing them together.

There were two principal kinds of foundations; one, and the better kind, was made of rocks and mud beginning at the bottom in a slight excavation and extending back as far as the hearth was intended to reach. This was continued upward until the level of the floor was reached where large flat rocks or fine white sand was used to make the hearth. Sometimes the rocks and mud would continue up to the jambs or the neck of the chimney, at which place the sticks of the frame began. The sticks were about two or three feet long and one or two inches square, arranged like the logs in a long pen.

The other kind was known as a sandbox. It was different only in the foundation underneath the hearth. This consisted of boards slanting from the floor down to the foot of the chimney proper, with boards on the side to case-in the sand that filled it. The usual objection to this type of foundation was the ease with which the rats could undermine them and endanger the house by allowing fire to penetrate their runs down to the boards.

Several advantages can be attributed to the stick-and-dirt chimney over one entirely of rocks and mud. It was more easily and quickly built, it was lighter, thus insuring safety from falling, and yet crude as the old timer might appear, he had a sense of beauty. No one wanted a rough and unsightly chimney that would result from the construction with rocks and mud alone. Whereas, the mud and sticks could be made into a perfect square or rectangular stack that would lend a much needed dignity to the old time cabin.

Most of the fireplaces had an iron bar across from the jamb to the other, to support the arch. On this was placed a hook on which could be hung pots for cooking. In the better homes a crane might be placed on an assembly on the jamb that would be swung back and forth over this fire as the housewife desired.

By Miss Lera [sic 'Lear'] Durbin,
Assistant Historian, C.W.A.,
Date: 1934.
Shiloh National Military Park,
Pittsburg Landing, Tennessee

Such may have been the typical handiwork of the Wicker's in 1848. This includes not only utilizing their "lesser family members" (Sarah, Mary and Elzina, ages 10-6) to prepare the rolls spoken of, but the same can be said for those later of the George family (their Sarah and Mary, ages 8 and 4) in post-battle 1862, when the cabin gets moved and "re-chinked." While considered work by the adults, one can envision the children of the two families at first, "oohing and aahing" at initially mixing the gooey mud and grass. Then, laughing as they eventually begin getting it on themselves which probably escalated to throwing it at each other, the adults chastising to stop them.

When first arriving in Hardin County and before any cabins were finished, where did the family sleep? Also, what was a survival tool? The following gives us some idea:

Depending on the season of the year, the members of a family might have slept in a lean-to of boughs, their wagon or a makeshift tent while their cabin was being built. Sometimes in areas where other families had arrived first and had completed their cabins, the newcomers shared a neighbor's dwelling until their own was raised...

No pioneer family could survive without an axe to fell trees and notch the logs for the cabin. It also served to clear the land for cornfields and pastures. It was used to cut through the roots that held the tree stumps in the earth, to cut wood to size for the fireplace and to split the rails and posts needed in fence building.[12]

Perry Field at the park entrance where the cabin first stood. Author photo.

Which fields did the Wicker's originally clear for the cabin or farming? Probably the future Perry Field, or the Russian Tenant Field or others to the north showing corn and cotton and plowed areas, on a pre-battle park map within the potential confines of Lewis Wicker's original 400 acres. Son

[12] Key, "The Pioneer Log Cabin."

Joseph and new wife Barbra's cabin was built on it as well. Did he carry his new bride across their home's threshold, if a tradition there?

All living there in cabins at that time, would have witnessed over the old Hamburg-Savannah Road the passing of passengers, cotton and produce, heading to Pittsburg Landing to boats going downstream.[13] In the previous picture, the author is standing on that old Hamburg-Savannah Road, on original Wicker-owned land, taking the photo.

Life for the Wicker's in the Old Cabin.

Lewis and Flora Wicker were quite well established as a farmer and housekeeper in Lincoln County, Tennessee, having been there some twenty years raising their large family before coming to Hardin County. Items needed to continue that lifestyle, where possible, would have been brought with them. Thereafter, descriptions by Miss Durbin of daily life in this period are quite apropos to define theirs. The following is the last page taken from a typed draft copy of her research paper notes, not used in the final paper, but photocopied from park files and computer transcribed here:

Clothes:

Girls and women worked at the spinning wheel. Girls learned to spin and knit early, and did their sewing by hand. The time for making clothes was all the time! Even when going to a neighbor's home to visit, women carried their spinning wheel along to spin as they visited. Little time was wasted. Baths were taken in a big wooden tub of water in front of the fireplace.

---

[13] Albert Dillahunty, *Shiloh National Military Park, Tennessee* (1955), National Park Service Historical Handbook Series No. 10, Washington, D. C., Reprinted 1961, http://www.nps.gov/history/history/online_books/hh/10/index.htm#top.

Woman spinning yarn[14]

Food:

They ate much corn – boiled corn and roasted corn, corn ground into corn meal and baked into corn cake, corn hoe cakes, corn pudding, grits and mush. They planted vegetables and fruit trees, especially cornstalk beans, and cooked them into mush or porridge. Men and boys fished in the Tennessee River and hunted in nearby woods, bringing fish, clams, rabbits, squirrels, bear and deer home to eat. Most families kept a few pigs so they could have bacon and pork and sausage; chickens too were kept for meat and eggs. Cows supplied meat and milk. Meat was smoked salted and pickled. Apples and pumpkins and peaches were peeled and sliced and hung up to dry to be cooked in stews or made into jams later. Jellies were made from berries and grapes gathered wild in the woods.

House:

The entire family worked hard; there was spinning and

---

[14] "Department of Conservation Photograph Collection, 1937-1976," *Tennessee Virtual Archive (TeVA)*, a program of the Tennessee State Library and Archives, http://tsla-teva.state.tn.us/.

weaving and knitting to be done. There were gardens to weed, rows and rows of corn to hoe, food to gather, prepare and cook; bread to bake, soap to make, butter to churn–no end to work. There were beds and tables and chairs and brooms and buckets and barrels to make. Fences had to be built and mended, fields plowed, cotton chopped and stock tended to.

Chair and broom makers[15]

Children worked with the adults but also played some games still played today; tag, blind man's bluff, sang "London Bridge is Falling Down" and "Here we go around the Mulberry Bush." Boy's played with a leather ball filled with feathers. They had tops to spin, drums to bang, popguns to pop, hoops to roll, marbles to shoot, kites to fly. Girls played mostly with dolls made of rags and cornhusks.

The family traveled rough and slow on roads like the Sunken Road on wagons and horses and oxen. Roads were narrow and bumpy and full of holes; dusty when dry, they became so muddy when it rained that wagon wheels could mire to hubcaps.

---

[15] Ibid.

Woman making cornhusk dolls[16]

This travel fact, of which she writes, not only the Wickers and other locals learned, but the Confederate troops of April 1862 discovered on their way to Shiloh from Corinth, Mississippi as their wagons and artillery bogged down after rain fell. During its tenure at two locations, the occupants of the old cabin, on and off over the years, would have both witnessed and experienced those conditions, on the roads associated with it.

Shiloh road crew in the late 1890's. Note the muddy conditions. Courtesy of Dr. Ronnie Fullwood[17]

---

[16] Ibid.

[17] Fullwood, *Shiloh's House of Peace,* 100.

Chapter 2: The 1850 Census and Land Transactions Document the Cabin

By the October 1850 census, Lewis had built his cabin, plus one for son Joseph who was living on the same land. In that census, the 10th Civil District was south of Snake Creek and west of the Tennessee River. Lewis Wicker and family were in the cabin that he built within what is today's entrance to Shiloh National Military Park, although more than one building may have been erected to accommodate the large family and their slave.

Lewis and family, living in their eventual historic log cabin, were the first dwelling house (number 1) to be visited by the census taker, coming from Savannah (post office in 1850) and crossing the Snake Creek Bridge to enter that district, a fact to be addressed later. Son Joseph and wife Barbra, mentioned earlier, were the second visited, all as follows:

Last Name	First Name	Age	Sex	Occup.	Val.	Birth-place
Wicker	Lewis	47	M	Farmer	937	NC
Wicker	Flora	46	F			NC
Wicker	Roderick G.	22	M	Laborer		NC
Wicker	Barthena	20	F			TN
Wicker	Matthew	17	M	Laborer		TN
Wicker	Andrew J.	16	M	Laborer		TN
Wicker	Lewis J.	14	M			TN
Wicker	Francis M.	12	M			TN
Wicker	Sarah A.	10	F			TN

Last Name	First Name	Age	Sex	Occup.	Val.	Birth-place
Wicker	Elisabeth	9	F			TN
Wicker	Elzina	6	F			TN
Wicker	Joseph C.	25	M	Farmer		NC
Wicker	Barbara C.	22	F			TN[18]

The fourth dwelling visited was that of John J. Ellis, a purchase grant holder whose ownership and land transactions will play into the Wicker's and the history of the old cabin. This is conveyed to recognize the close proximity then of these two land owners.

For the sake of the old cabin's future history, it is necessary to report 1850 census data for the eventual marriage that connected the Bell-George family that occurred about 1852. Living further south of Wicker and Ellis in the same census district is Sarah Bell, already the widow of Samuel Bell. Living at home with Sarah is sixteen year-old daughter Nancy J. ("Jane") and future wife (about 1852) of William Mansfield George.

At this time, the closest this author came to finding him in the 1850 census is as an eighteen-year-old William George with a Thomas B. George in Lincoln County, Tennessee, where the Wicker's came from. However, there are several Georges in McNairy County that is next to Hardin County, so one may be his family. William M. George and Wicker son, Alvis, whether together is unknown, both came to Hardin shortly after the 1850 census as they quickly thereafter married Hardin girls, coincidentally living next door to each other, in that census.

Alvis left Lincoln County, probably after the fall harvest and census of 1850, as he had enough time to meet and

[18] Roseanne Cain, transcription, "1850 Census for Hardin County," *Hardin County, Tennessee History & Genealogy*, http://ftp.rootsweb.ancestry.com/pub/usgenweb/tn/hardin/census/1850/ (USGenWeb).

marry his Hardin gal, obviously some months before December of 1851, when their first child, John W. Wicker, was born (He will grow up and buy land the old cabin is on in 1885). Alvis married Susan Stacy, who, along with her widowed mother Nancy, was a neighbor to Sarah Bell in 1850. Importantly, apparently Alvis and Susan built a third cabin on Wicker land by 1851, as three buildings end up there.

Another significant event occurred by the December of 1851 date for the Wicker family. Lewis has his first recorded sale deed for twenty-two acres in his southwest corner. As we will see, it did not contain the old original cabin. He sold the acreage to neighbor John J. Ellis, possibly for money, or, because Ellis desired better access to his adjacent acres, which wrapped around Wickers on three sides, as shown later.

In turn, Ellis later sold the same twenty-two acres in early 1853 to James A. Perry, along with most of Ellis's original purchase grant acres. Then near the end of 1853, Wicker deeded his remaining 378 acres to Allen G. Kendrick, wealthy landowner to the south in that district, thereby passing the cabin land ownership. Although the twenty-two acres sold to Ellis in December 1851 may have included a Wicker-built cabin, Lewis's family did not move to the future "Wicker Field," until or after, he sold the 378 acres two years later in November, 1853. This is because that deed stated the land as "being the farm on which the said Wicker now lives." So, Wicker was still living in his original cabin when he sold Kendrick the last of his farm acreage.

Lewis may not have liked his 378 acres, some of which is bottom land, near where Owl Creek joins Snake Creek and is subject to flooding. According to park contour maps, the highest part of his land dropped over eighty feet towards the confluence of the two creeks, at the point Lewis's land ended. We can know this because when Kendrick later sold what the deed referred to as "the Wicker place" (the 378 acres) to Mr. Perry in 1855, that deed stated the land was "about the mouth of Owl Creek and on Snake Creek."

It also includes a neighboring property in the sale, "the McWhirter place." The deed for both pieces includes a reference to a "Range 6 & Section 2 & 3," used in legal descriptions, and refers to them as, "two certain tracts of land." It has been proven by deed research that James A. Perry eventually owned over a thousand connected acres in this area, including all of Wicker's and most of Ellis's entry land. Later, G. W. Tilghman will own some of it in the early 1870's and eventually sell it to the USA for the park.

For Wicker, Ellis, Kendrick, Perry and Tilghman deeds, this author has transcribed and plotted them out with overlaps and adjacent-to-one-another ownerships, and although connected, they are a floating island at this time with no definite tie point. That includes Wicker's original 400 acres. However, since Lewis was listed first on the 1850 census in Civil District 10 (south of Snake Creek), that reinforces the following. Based on where the cabin was, the beginning of his acreage was at the southeasterly corner of today's park entrance, known as Perry Field, and runs west for about three-quarters of a mile, then north for about a mile (to near the creeks), then east three-quarters of a mile and south to the point of beginning.

Perry eventually owned all on the following map, except the larger dashed area (Ellis kept it); Wicker land was in the center, Ellis land was south and west (wraps around Wicker's), the smaller dashed line area is Wicker to Ellis to Perry to Tilghman, then the rest of Wicker's to Kendrick then to Perry. Perry's son sold all of the land his father bought from Ellis, to Tilghman just after 1870. The older Perry also owned the northeast piece – the 'McWhirter place' bought from Kendrick, as mentioned already (The broken lines on the graph indicate, that ownership runs further north than shown). Of the above landowners doing business, Kendrick and Ellis are dead by 1860; soon after, Perry and Wicker.

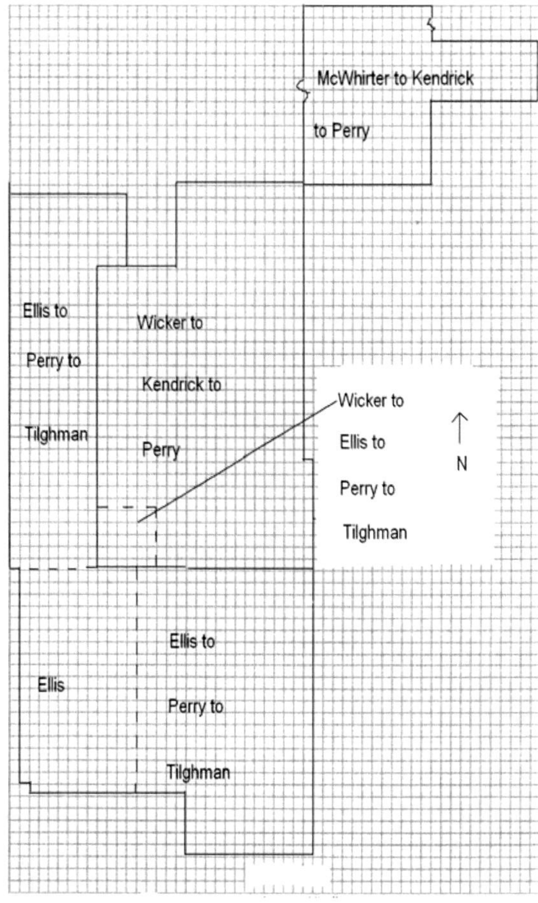

1848-1871 land holdings near today's park entrance and running north

In summary, Lewis' recorded deeds selling all his acreage, occurring in late 1851 and 1853, confirm his ownership of what was previously a part of the Chickasaw Cession. This accounts for all 400 acres of Lewis Wicker's original land, beginning at the park entrance in what is known as Perry Field, and running north. This is the field that park history says the cabin survived the battle on, and then was bought and relocated from to its present location, near "Bloody Pond" and adjacent to the "Peach Orchard."

As today's Tour Stop Number 13 in the park, Albert Dillahunty, National Park Service Historian, says the following on the "War Cabin" in his book from the 1950's on Shiloh:

This cabin formerly stood in Perry Field on the Federal right and in the immediate front of the last Union line established on Sunday afternoon, the first day of the battle. The battle-scarred logs revealed that it stood in the midst of heavy fighting. Of the many cabins on the field at the time of the battle, this is the only survivor. The cabin was moved to the present location, a few weeks after the battle, to replace one that was burned during the engagement.[19]

The 'War Cabin' in 1934.
Courtesy of Shiloh National Military Park (SNMP)

[19] Dillahunty, *Shiloh*, 32.

The historic original cabin location reported by the park, on today's Perry Field, and the reference to Wicker Field adjacent to Bloody Pond, plus deed research and plotting, led to not initially understanding why the two didn't match? This author was told in his Texas-growing-up-youth by his mother, Wanda (Montgomery) Helweg, who heard it directly from her grandmother, Mary Lucrecia (Wicker) Strawn/Montgomery, that Wicker lands and homes were involved in the middle of the Civil War Battle of Shiloh.

It is difficult to reconcile Wicker's original land ownership location and what is known today as Wicker Field. There is a viable theory, however, based on what can be known or what seems to be. Allen Kendrick lived further south in the 10th district in 1850 and is shown to be a "C of C clergyman" per that census. He has considerable wealth and land for those days. Lewis was getting older and his boys were leaving home to marry.

When Lewis sold his acreage he may have struck a deal either by handshake, or even written, to have Kendrick allow Lewis's family to move onto some of Kendrick's holding's further south, as in the future "Wicker Field." Kendrick owned this site as eventually his widow, Nancy, sold it to James J. Fraley, as detailed later. The Wicker's apparently simply became tenants and in turn agreed to share part of anything produced there, or, the boys may have provided wild game for Kendrick's table. Even if such were in writing, it would not ordinarily be recorded. The Wickers will now be neighbors to William Mansfield 'Manse' and Nancy (Bell) George, future movers/owners of the cabin.

Based on the timing and wording of all the above, it is apparent that sometime after the sale of his remaining land in November of 1853, Lewis and family (including Joseph but not Alvis) vacated his farm and at least two of their three cabins. They then either built new ones, or used existing ones, and occupied what was to become known, in Civil War infamy, and, in today's Shiloh National Military Park, as "Wicker Field."

If one visits the park today and either speaks to rangers there or looks at or purchases a park map, you will see privately named fields throughout the park. These are all also mentioned at one time or another in the myriad of accounts written about battle history.

At one time the park even had small name plates displayed on a pole at each location. Up until about ten years ago the farmers who leased the fields could grow row crops like corn, soybeans etc. to harvest (now it's hay only, like fescue grass).[20] They probably knocked the signs down with their plowing efforts, or, visiting park souvenir hunters just took them. There is also one named "Wicker Field" next to Bloody Pond, but this is not any of the original acreage owned by Lewis Wicker. However, it is the source of the park and battle history accounts referring to "Widow Wicker." Although Lewis, as a tenant, is alive at census time in October of 1860, he is apparently dead by April of 1862, thus his wife, Flora Wicker, is the widow referred to in accounts and battle references.

Sign like those once marking all field names. Author's photo.

[20] Dr. Ronnie Fullwood, land lessee at the park, e-mail message to author, September 6, 2007.

What that October 1860 census shows, as to the number of Wicker dwellings on or near the future named Wicker Field, confirms some oral family history, which includes who may have later sold the old cabin. Mary Lucrecia, known to some in Texas as "Crece," told her 2nd oldest daughter, Ida, stories about Shiloh, who shared it with her granddaughter, Cindy Mclaughlin. With this author's bracketed inserts, Cindy wrote:

Did I ever make it clear that Lewis and Flora Wicker (Crece's paternal grandparents) lived on a farm that is now part of the Shiloh Battlefield itself? Originally there was a group of about four cabins/houses in a compound, with barns and outbuildings. After the War [battle], Widow Flora sold at least one of them [maybe from Perry Field], which was moved to another property and still exists...Ida use to say that her Mother could remember the sounds and smells of the Battle of Shiloh. She was 8 years old at the time. She said that for two days they could not leave the cabin, and sometimes had to lie on the floor to avoid stray bullets. Crece would also say that some of her uncles [and her father] never came back from the war, and that the family never knew what happened to them [Three disappear].

Although the upcoming 1860 census will show Alvis as the only Wicker still living in the north part of that district, presumably still in a third cabin built there, James Perry owns the land it is on. He and his son are probably living in the other two now vacated Wicker-built cabins there, as the Perry's are censused in the north part of the district in 1860 also. James Perry, who is in nearby McNairy County in the previous 1850 census, began buying land thereafter in Hardin County but earlier than Wicker sold his holdings. However, as stated, Perry eventually bought "the Wicker place" by 1855.

Chapter 3: The 1860 Census – Neighbors

By 1860, three family names have become neighbors in the now 15th Civil District; Wicker's, Bell's and George's, and are about to become tied to the old cabin that remains elsewhere on the future Perry Field. Listed in the census were: William M. George (future cabin owner), age 28, wife Nancy J., age 25 and children Sarah S., age 5 and one-year-old Mary A. George; nearby are his widowed mother-in-law Sarah Bell, with three grown sons, plus next door the Hargroves, with son Robert, who, after the war and next census, will court and then marry the above Sarah George, while she is then living in the now moved former Wicker cabin; also listed are the Cantrell's, Duncan's, Barne's and McCuller's. Some are well known names documented in the battle history. These private names, and others, were used after the battle to identify the various military locations that set up and changed on farm fields or around homes during the two-day battle itself.

Although neighbor Lewis Wicker didn't die until after the census but before the battle, mentioned in historical battle accounts are "Widow Wicker" and "Wicker Field," as are "Widow Sarah Bell" and her "Old Cotton Field" and to-be-famous "Peach Orchard," plus, the future to-be-named "Bloody Pond" that existed between the three families. Although spring fed, the pond may not have been a source for household water as apparently water wells were dug to supply those needs, as shown by the following:

In the pre-war period, people tried to build near a spring, but it was not always possible to do this, and many homesteads had to have a well. This was the case at the [future site of the] "War Cabin." The well was located in the "Peach Orchard" between the home of Mr. George and Mrs. Bell.[21]

Five Wicker-related families lived either on or at least near, the future "Wicker Field" and members of each household were former builders/occupants of the old cabin, still existing elsewhere. For Lewis and Flora, only youngest child and teenager, Elzina, remained at home in 1860. Next door was their then widower son Matthew Wicker and his two children. Then the census lists two Wicker daughters; Sarah and Parthena (or Barthena), each married to a William, one surnamed Edwards and another Barnes, respectively, in two other households, each with their children. Finally, oldest son Joseph C. and wife "Barbry" (Hagy) Wicker were enumerated, along with their three children.

No doubt young neighbors Sarah and Mary George played with the above children. Also, both before and after the move of the old cabin, Widow Sarah Bell and Flora Wicker may have spun yarn or visited together, even before Flora became a widow by battle time. These two probably remained friends from as early as the Wicker arrival in the neighborhood in about 1853, through the early 1870's. These interactions of neighbors could have led to a future connection between the Wicker's and George's as to the purchase and move of the old cabin after the battle.

Flora and Lewis's son, Alvis Wicker, was living northwest of them near Owl and Snake Creeks, with wife

[21] Wicker, John, Personal Interview, 1934, footnoted by Lear Durbin, Assistant Historian, Civil Works Administration, Shiloh National Military Park, TN, "The 'War Cabin'– It's History and Proposed Construction" (Research paper, SNMP, April, 1934), author Duane Helweg's italicized brackets.

Susan and their four children. It appears that Alvis has remained on the future Perry Field in the 1860 census, near or next door to the old cabin in his own, built there probably by 1851. As mentioned, his census number is in the north part of today's park near James Perry, his son J. A. J. Perry, and, the Hagy family numbers.

As stated earlier, Perry Field was where the cabin survived the battle, near today's park entrance. Perry owned a great deal of land there, beginning in early 1853. Historic base maps for April 6-7, 1862 show three buildings on Perry Field and all three could be Wicker-built cabins; the original built by Lewis by 1849, then Joseph's by 1850, and last, Alvis's by 1852. As stated, by 1860, Lewis and Joseph are on the future Wicker Field.

(See Appendix #3 for historic base map)

Three other children of Lewis and Flora lived even further north, in District 11 above Snake Creek. One was, Roderick Wicker (this author's ancestor), who along with wife Catherine had three children. Another one of Lewis and Flora's sons, Lewis J., is known as "Jasper" in the 1860 census and he and wife Mahaly live to the north near Roderick. So does their sister, Mary Elizabeth, married to C. C. (Christopher Columbus) Strawn, with their two children. These Wicker adult children are all original cabin builders/occupants and are all documented here for the following reference regarding the old cabin.

These families above Snake Creek would have crossed the bridge on the old Hamburg-Savannah Road and either visited Alvis in his home near the old family cabin, or at least passed by it on the future Perry Field on their way to see their parents (and grandparents) on the also future Wicker Field. The memory of that original cabin and its history would no doubt have been verbally conveyed to their children as they passed by or stopped at it.

While all of these families in 1860 are documented because of their past, future and potential interactions with the cabin, both pre-move and post-move, it is not known, who, if anybody for sure was censused in it in 1860. It may have already lain empty by then and by battle time, seventeen months later. This author has and does speculate some on it.

Were Cabins Considered Real Estate?

There is some consideration that cabin ownership, in some instances, may not have always passed with the land, especially where tenancy is involved. The Wicker's censused in Civil District 15 in 1860 did not own any real estate except Lewis, and his was minor, valued at $150, perhaps only his cabin (or one on Perry Field if he moved into an existing one on the future Wicker Field), as they were tenants. Everyone had personal estate figures and Lewis' figure there was quite high. Of course he sold considerable land in 1853, and had two female slaves in the 1860 census (in their own cabin).

There is validity to addressing this small money amount real estate value (as opposed to personal property value) for some in the 1850 through 1870 census times. In the personal work experience of the author, real estate usually involves land ownership plus anything permanently attached to that land such as a house. In the above era, cabins were movable.

In the census eras mentioned, real estate meant land ownership for sure. Personal property might include anything used in your vocation, even farming. Certainly in the 1850 and 1860 censuses personal property values also meant the worth of any slaves owned. Now having said all that, it remains something of a mystery as to what a small real estate value meant in those early censuses? In speculating about it, other historians or knowledgeable sources have been canvassed.

The one idea, which some have agreed with, is that, for

those who were in tenancy upon the lands on which they lived, if they built their cabin or cabins and other potentially removable buildings, those may have represented real estate, and thus the small value. Based on per-acre value research of land in these census eras, and, the fact those showing such little real estate value never having a recorded deed, it points to a value of buildings built and owned, not land. Cabins could be taken down and moved.

Not that this was an every day practice but we know from the old original Wicker cabin itself, that it was movable, as Mr. George does later in 1862. Others had that same potential. In studying census history, both there in Tennessee and here in Texas, people tended to move around. This was brought about by size of family and economic needs. This may explain a small real estate value, such as Lewis Wicker had in 1860, Flora in 1870 and could have included their keeping cabin ownership, even back on Perry Field, especially if potentially occupied by one of their adult children.

Here's what the National Park Service Preservation Brief 26 says in defining log cabins. The defining words underlined are "somewhat impermanent" which, although primarily meaning "to not last long," contributes to the idea of being able to move them:

"…'Log cabin' generally denotes a simple one, or one-and-one-half story structure, somewhat impermanent, and less finished or less architecturally sophisticated."[22]

[22] Bruce D. Bomberger, "The Preservation and Repair of Historic Log Buildings," National Park Service Preservation Brief 26, http://www.nps.gov/history/hps/tps/briefs/brief26.htm.

Chapter 4:
The Coming Civil War

After the census in Hardin County in late October of 1860 and with the soon coming Civil War, life was about to dramatically change for all the families at Shiloh. A mere seventeen months, and April 6th, 1862 would become a "Black Sunday." Travail was just beginning for some households. Their homes and lives would be in peril, but the old cabin will survive the coming end of some of its counterparts.

The first sign of impending doom may have been the enrollment of husband's, fathers, son's and son-in-laws, or future ones, into various Confederate/Union regiments by 1861. Those of the Wicker family are detailed below to show the potential loss of family lives, and, how brother was pitted against brother in this controversial cause. "In this battle neighbor often faced neighbor, brother faced brother, and boys who had been playmates from youth and classmates in school met here to put an end to each other's existence."[23] Even Hardin County had split sides; east of the Tennessee…Union, west…Confederate:

"There is a terrible war coming, and these young men who have never seen war cannot wait for it to happen, but I tell you, I wish that I owned every slave in the South, for I would free them all to avoid this war." - Robert E. Lee [24]

---

[23] B. G. Brazelton, *A History of Hardin County, Tennessee* (unnumbered).
[24] General Robert E. Lee, quoted in *Tennessee and the Civil War*, http://www.tngenweb.org/civilwar.

Soldier Name	Side	Function	Regiment Name
Wicker, Joseph	Confederate	Infantry	34th Regiment, Tennessee Infantry
Wicker, A.M.	Confederate	Infantry	23rd Battalion, Tennessee Infantry (Newman's)
Wickar, R.G.	Confederate	Artillery	Phillip's Company, Tennessee Light Artillery
Wicker, Mathew	Confederate	Infantry	34th Regiment, Tennessee Infantry
Wicker, Jasper	Union	Cavalry	6th Regiment, Tennessee Cavalry
Barnes, William C.	Confederate	Infantry	34th Regiment, Tennessee Infantry
Edwards, William	Confederate	Artillery	Phillip's Company, Tennessee Light Artillery
Strawn, C.C.	Confederate	Cavalry	16th Regiment, Tennessee Cavalry
Green, Dennis	Confederate	Infantry	31st Regiment, Tennessee Infantry
Strawn, John	Confederate	Artillery	Phillip's Company, Tennessee Light Artillery [25]

Then in early 1862 the blue cloud of the Union Army swept down upon the 15th Civil District residents. Shortly, the rest is history, as they say. The daily lives and by-products of their living were dismantled and lost, save for some of the battle-periphery log cabins.

The day of the Union army arrival, what conversation took place at the supper table that evening if the old cabin was occupied (or any cabin); what fears, what dread, what surmising? Did they know what was taking place, or about to? Was a wife expressing fears for her children, the man of the

[25] National Park Service, *Civil War Soldiers and Sailors System*, http://www.itd.nps.gov/cwss.

house trying to assuage those fears but all the time fearing himself; the harm to family, the loss of food, the eventual loss of his own life? What were the soldiers doing there? How long were they going to stay? Would the Confederate side show up someday? What must we do to stay safe? Can life go on here as usual? If only the walls of the old cabin could talk, knowing its future…their future.

What was the effect on the locals in west Hardin County, of the Union troop's arrival? Were their children in fear or fascinated by the event? Probably both, as the following shows; this author's mother conveyed a story, which shall be contributed to the spunk of a young eight-year-old Mary Lucrecia Wicker, at battle time. Perhaps it can be attributed to her part Iroquois blood that not only gave her beauty but backbone as well.

Mary Lucrecia Wicker; pre-1874 tin-type reproduction

The story goes that in the Civil War, before or after Shiloh, the Union soldiers came to procure food. "Crece" peeked from behind her mother's (or Grandmother Flora's?) long skirt and proudly announced, "You won't find our food 'cause we hid it under the floor!" Maybe she was in or near the old cabin before the battle, or even afterwards before it was moved, when she made that revealing, costly statement. Other local reactions follow:

War came to the civilians in Hardin County, Tennessee, in the spring of 1862. What had been a matter for public debate and far away confrontations came upriver with the huge

Federal army, disembarking at the foot of Main Street in Savannah and about eight miles south at a small landing called Pittsburg. Theoretical political divisions between friends became matters of life and death, homes were disrupted throughout the county, and nothing would ever be the same again. Three groups of civilians saw the war from the closest possible perspective—the people of Savannah, the people of the Pittsburg Landing area, and the northern citizens who either accompanied the transports south, or who came to aid the wounded immediately after the battle of Shiloh.

Even after fighting had begun, much of Savannah and the eastern part of the county continued to quietly support the old flag, while the western side of the river tended to be pro-Confederate. The militia began to drill, and in the summer of 1861 Confederates held a recruiting "grand barbecue" west of Saltillo, with patriotic speeches and a mounted parade around the camp meeting arbor by enlistees "with small flags attached to their horses' heads." Charles S. Robertson soon formed a cavalry company, followed by the "Hardin County Boys," Company B, 34th Tennessee Infantry. Officials instituted a local draft for additional men and from those Col. Crews formed a five-company regiment, armed with confiscated squirrel rifles and double-barrel shotguns, clothed with home-produced brown jeans cloth uniforms with a black stripe running down each pant leg. This unit would guard the county seat. The Southern cause was at its zenith in Hardin County.[26]

Then another view about the effects of war on civilians:

Civil War historians...write volumes about military movements and great generals; they chronicle the simple soldier and his version of "seeing the elephant," his initiation into battle. But characteristically, they tend to ignore the

[26] Vicki Betts, "A Revelation of War: Civilians in Hardin County, Tennessee, Spring, 1862," http://www.uttyler.edu/vbetts/shiloh.htm.

civilian populace, the landowners who called the battlefields home, the parents who soldiers left behind, and the folks that merely peopled the landscape...The life of the Southern civilian was often just as dangerous and as full of despair as any soldier's. With many goods in short supply, with invading armies scavenging the countryside, the war on the home front was not measured by battles and skirmishes, but by the grueling, heartbreaking, day-to-day chore of simple survival. One group of Hardin County civilians saw their own special breed of the elephant very early in the war, before the rest of the country realized the tragedy ahead. They were among the first to witness the carnage of war, among the first to have their innocence shattered. They were the people who called Shiloh 'home.'[27]

As reported in Wiley Sword's, *Shiloh: Bloody April*, did the 'sutlers' (or those who followed and privately sold to gathering and marching armies[28]) who arrived at Shiloh to sell tobacco and canned fruit, etc., to the army, sell to the locals as well? Interestingly, he also reported that the local population on the west side of the river apparently never confided to the Union that the Confederates had marched and gathered before the battle.[29]

In the *'Official Records,'*[30] Union Brig.-Gen. Sherman gave Col. Buckland these instructions on April 3, 1862. "Do

---

[27] Staff Writer, "The Civil War Comes to Hardin County, TN," *Savannah Courier*.

[28] *Dictionary and Thesaurus - Merriam-Webster Online*, http://www.merriam-webster.com/.

[29] Wiley Sword, *Shiloh: Bloody April* (Dayton, OH: Morningside House, 2001), 35, 352.

[30] War Department, *The War of the Rebellion: a Compilation of the Official Records of the Union and Confederate Armies*, Series 1 – Vol. 10 (Part I), (Washington DC: GPO, 1884), Cornell University Library, http://cdl.library.cornell.edu/cgi-bin/moa/sgml/moa-idx?notisid=ANU4519-0010, 90.

not molest people quietly at their usual occupation as farmers, mechanics, but all persons armed, uniformed, or suspicious bring in as prisoners." [Any future references to *'OR'* is short for the above *'Official Records,'* Series 1 – Vol. 10 (Part I) on Shiloh]

In a report in the *'OR'* by the Union's Lt. Col. John A. Rawlins about Lew Wallace's march to Shiloh the first battle day, he says, "...we met some citizens...who informed us that the bridge across Snake Creek was in possession of the enemy." [31] It wasn't true but it delayed them more. Those indications show that side of Hardin County being Southern.

In the Hargrove/Bell/George histories, a family member reported that Sarah George told "about her childhood memories of Union gunboats coming up the Tennessee River to their town [Pittsburg Landing]."[32] From the Bell history but confirmed by the Hargrove history as well, it says: "Manse and Nancy's great granddaughter has a silver goblet that Nancy buried before the Yankees came."[33] It was dug up after the battle or upon their return. This is a true story as this author has spoken to this descendant who still has the goblet that was once buried in the yard where the park's old cabin now stands.

Goblet buried before the battle, at the present cabin site. Courtesy of the owner.

[31] War Department, *Official Records*, 187.

[32] Dorothy Hargrove Hogan, "Hargrove History," courtesy of Larry DeBerry.

[33] Gaye Granger Stokes, "The Bell Family at Shiloh," courtesy of Larry DeBerry.

Detailed is the Wicker family and others in the 1860 census because it impacts both the factual history and the speculative ones made by this author on fact-based deductions, as necessary, regarding the cabin history. Two Wicker family stories come out of the pre-battle and battle days themselves and both involve original cabin builder/occupants:

The first is a love story uncovered through an Internet connection made by Cindy Mclaughlin. It is about Lewis and Flora's youngest daughter, Elzina (or Eliza). In an e-mail to Cindy, a relative of an Irish-born Confederate soldier, Dennis Green, shares this:

My uncle told me that D. Green was with some troops, and that they found Eliza and three other children hiding on the bank of the Owl Creek and that they gave them a pass to leave the field before the battle. And that after the war was over, D. Green came back and married Eliza.

Being a Confederate in Union held territory, up until at least the first day of battle, it's unsure when "Sergeant Green" offered or gave them a safe passage through, presumably, military lines. However, he apparently was awestruck by the teenager, Elzina. So much so that he returned after the war and married her in Hardin County, Tennessee as a June bride named as "Eliza." on the marriage record, the eighth day of June, 1865. After the war, Dennis wasted no time in returning to court the now older "lass," living next door to the old now moved cabin, she no doubt his shining ray of hope on each waking war day.

At battle time, did Elzina and the children leave or were sent for protection from, or near, the old cabin that survived on Perry Field, if Alvis lived there? Alvis and Susan had four children under age ten at battle time, the youngest only about two. Teenaged Aunt Elzina could easily be the baby sitter for the older three, with the youngest still in its mother's possession to feed. Alvis' infantry unit did not organize until November of 1862, after Shiloh, so whether he was home and stayed behind with Susan and sent Elzina and the older kids out earlier, is unknown. It leads us to the other family story of Roderick Gaines Wicker.

This second family story concerns the battle itself. While none of the named family soldiers units were officially recognized as being at Shiloh, it is believed some members were there. If you were aware of, or were home on leave, or hadn't reported for duty yet and several thousand Union troops were camped in your back yard, threatening your homes and families security, where would you be, if at all possible? Not to mention the potential to be invaluable to the Rebel troops and officers ready to move up from Corinth, Mississippi. Locals, such as the Wickers, would know the area like the back of their hands. You would also want to defend your homes and families, if a battle was brewing.

Here's the story of one such situation. It is believed Roderick died in the battle, not only from a verbal indication by this author's mother but also per the following oral story e-mailed by a family member. Roderick (plus brother-in-law William Edwards mentioned previously) and a young unmarried neighbor, John Strawn, joined Phillips's Light Artillery Company for the war. Here is the Strawn history as passed down, with this author's comments in brackets:

As the story goes, Strawn [John] and Wicker [Roderick]...fought together as Confederate "Flag Bearers" in the Civil War Battle of Shiloh which was fought on their property [other Wicker family, but near Strawns]. Wicker was shot, fell, and Strawn grabbed the flag to hold it upright. Wicker asked Strawn to take care of his wife and children. Strawn replied that with Wicker's permission, he would marry the daughter (Mary Lucrecia), and take care of the family, as best he could. Wicker agreed just before dying.

The war record was obtained for R. G. "Wickar" from the National Archives in Washington. To this author's surprise, his only muster roll record showed him "deserted" as of May 16, 1862 while stationed at Corinth, Mississippi. In researching his unit's history at the Tennessee State Library, that date was their first muster roll record covering December 31, 1861 to April 30, 1862. It stated, "This Company was on detached service and was not mustered until today." It was dated May 16, 1862. John Strawn, plus Wicker son-in-law William Edwards, individual records show them "absent on detached service" so they were not at Corinth that day to tell them what happened to Roderick back on April 6th or 7th. Had he previously been on detached service to Shiloh and died there?

Chief Park Ranger Stacy Allen looked at the military history of Phillips Light Artillery and discovered a four month record gap between January 1862 and May 1862 when in Corinth. He believes they may have been without artillery guns during that time and therefore some could have been detached and at Shiloh. It is also worthy to show that noted in the company's history it says, "On January 31, 1862, it was placed in Colonel John S. Bowen's Brigade, Brigadier General John B. Floyd's Division, of Major General Hardee's command."[34] Both Bowen and Hardee were at Shiloh, per the *'OR'*.[35]

The Wicker family believes the above story of Roderick to be true, as Mary Lucrecia Wicker, at age fifteen, did marry John Strawn in 1868 in Hardin County. That means Roderick "deserted" because he was dead weeks earlier, by April 7th, and probably lies buried in a mass Confederate grave on the field of Shiloh. Did he die on a farm or near remaining cabins, even the one on Perry Field that he helped build and live in initially? If there on "detached service" was he "attached" to Ketchum's

---

[34] "Captain J. W. Phillips' Tennessee Light Artillery Company, 'Johnston Light Artillery,'" *Tennesseans in the Civil War, Confederate Artillery Units*, http://www.tngenweb.org/civilwar/csaart/phillips.html.
[35] War Department, *Official Records*, 383-384.

unit, as detailed later? If so, was he the one "bowled over" by the Union artillery early Monday in the battle?

How were the dead mourned during and in post-Civil War days? Some idea can be taken from the following, with this author's underlining:

The Civil War ushered in death on a level never experienced by the American psyche. With a collective loss of nearly 620,000 men in four years, nearly every American was impacted by family deaths, deaths of friends and neighbors, and by mentally and physically damaged veterans who returned home. But mourning no longer meant just mourning for the dead. <u>It meant mourning the loss of homes, income, and a way of life for thousands</u>. The grief of civilians also extended beyond private grief to grieving for public disasters such as lost battles, dead military heroes, and later, fallen cities in the South. The overwhelming losses caused Americans to rethink mourning clothing and rituals, and in some cases, they were abandoned altogether.[36]

Local, Sallie White, at Ledbetter Cemetery, near Shiloh, showing burials.

[36] Karen Rae Mehaffey, "Mourning the Dead: Stages of Mourning for the Bereaved," *Citizen's Companion, The Voice of Civilian Reenacting*, Morristown, TN, http://www.citizenscompanion.com/news/view_sections.asp?idcategory=9&idarticle=378.

Chapter 5:
What Did The Cabin Experience Sunday, April 6, 1862?

As a preface to what the area of the cabin on Perry Field was subjected to at battle time, the following was received by e-mail from Chief Park Ranger Stacy Allen:

The cabin witnessed its own unique share of history, but was not involved in the greater part of the combat–which occurred well beyond Perry Field. The location of the structure being beyond or on the extreme edge of the intense combat is the primary reason it survived the battle and still extant (although in rough condition) in 1895 when the War Department Battlefield Commission began the task of preserving the battlefield and related surviving features–otherwise the old building would have suffered the fate of the vast majority of structures caught within the main firestorm of battle, which were either destroyed outright or so heavily damaged as a result of the combat to be beyond repair.[37]

Because the old cabin was apparently unoccupied at some point after the battle and therefore available to be sold and moved, initial logic would say it was also possibly vacant before the Union even arrived. However, based on census

[37] Chief Park Ranger Stacy Allen, e-mail message to author, May 2007.

records both before and after the war, Alvis Mathis Wicker apparently still occupied a cabin, one of three buildings on Perry Field. And since his Confederate unit did not organize until after Shiloh in late 1862, then he would have been at home, when, as stated previously, "the blue cloud of the Union Army swept down upon the 15th Civil District residents."

Therefore, Alvis and his family would have witnessed and endured the Federal encampments all around Perry Field. Whoever the cabin occupants, if any, they would have been aware of the Union camp of Hare across Tilghman Branch to the west. Along the Hamburg-Savannah Road to the north were the units of McArthur's Brigade, while the other portions of W.H.L. Wallace's command lay encamped to the north and east - the brigades under Sweeny and Tuttle. The brigade under Veatch assigned to Hurlbut's Division, was encamped south and east of Perry Field.[38]

This is as it was at 4:55 A.M. on the Sunday morning of April 6, 1862, another Sabbath day for the soul, but a Devil's dues to pay for some, before it's over. Some citizens remained afield when the battle started. As Chief Ranger Allen stated, "Where else would they be?" According to him, some dispersed south behind Confederate lines, others to the north behind the Union lines. The Wickers probably went north of Snake Creek to family.

The Hezekiah Pickens family, living in the southern battle area as neighbors to the Seay, Fraley and Howell families, went south, as reported in a newspaper article in 1939 in Texas. The interviewer stated that, "News of the approaching Battle of Shiloh drove them to move up [south] the Tennessee River about two miles from the scene of the battle."[39] Later on is a detail of one family who apparently even

[38] Stacy D. Allen, Historian, Shiloh National Military Park, "Shiloh!," *Blue & Gray, A Visitor's Guide*, 2001.

[39] Newspaper interview of Mrs. A. V. Carothers, Sylvester, Fisher County, Texas, 1939. Joanne Baucum, e-mail message to author, August 14, 2007.

remained at home the entire time, on the fringe of the battlefield, not far from Perry Field, their cabin hit once by shell.

Were there occupants in the cabins on Perry Field at this hour and time? Or did the story of Elzina Wicker and three children hiding on Owl Creek occur some 2-3 days before, during Confederate reconnaissance? Whether the cabins were occupied or empty, and whether or not their location and the terrain and topography allowed witnessing it, at a given point the battle erupted elsewhere with first the sounds of Shiloh, then adding the sights and smells, all coming together eventually in a chorus never before sung, smelled or seen, by the likes of witness…cabin or otherwise.

First the crack and pop of musketry, the roar of cannon and the yells of men, whether out of fear or fierceness, joined by the sight of smoke and smell of spent powder and view of men, artillery and horses in battle. That would quickly turn to death and destruction, wounds and war moans, blood baths and battle blight. The cabin itself would eventually suffer its own war wounds on that day or the next; bullet holes from round or minie (pronounced 'mi-nē'[40]) balls and perhaps shrapnel from canister shot, but saved from cannonballs themselves, and, fate of fire itself upon its wooden carcass; all means that wiped out many of its log counterparts elsewhere in the battleground proper.

Interestingly, in searching through the *'OR,'* which can easily be done online at the Cornell University web site, there are report entries referencing "cabins." A simple-search of the appropriate volume for Shiloh (Volume 10), using such terms as 'log,' together with, or singularly, 'cabin,' 'house,' 'building,' etc. will find instances both battle days, from either side, which included; firing artillery at a cabin, a burning cabin, sharpshooters at a cabin, officer headquarters (other than the

[40] *Dictionary and Thesaurus - Merriam-WebsterOnline.*

one at Pittsburg Landing itself or Shiloh Church) at cabins and finally, the wounded placed within or about cabins.

Following is a synopsis of times and positions, relative to the cabin on Perry Field, taken from: Stacy D. Allen, Historian, Shiloh National Military Park, "Shiloh!," *Blue & Gray, A Visitor's Guide*, 2001. Further special editing and contributions on some portions of the following are by Chief Park Ranger Stacy Allen, in an e-mail message to the author, May 2007, and are attributed to "Chief Ranger Allen," accordingly:

The first musketry shots occurred at 4:55 A.M., some three miles southwest of Perry Field and the cabin. Shortly after 7:00 A.M. the first artillery fire occurs. Anyone near the cabin may not have heard the first shots but certainly would the artillery fire. Some reports are that the battle could eventually be heard as far as 25 miles away.[41] Another local description from, Eliza Hill, who lived near Purdy in next door McNairy County was that, "It sounded to her like the pouring of dried peas onto a dried cowhide."[42]

Chief Ranger Allen:

The Federals in this vicinity [Perry Field and the cabin] understood by 8:00 A.M. that the front line organizations occupying the Pittsburg Landing encampment were under general attack. Hurlbut sent Veatch marching southwest from his camps to reinforce Sherman and McClernand by 8:10 A.M., and [W.H.L.] Wallace's units, forming on their camp color lines at 8:00 A.M., began to file southward by 8:30 A.M. Union troops began to retreat/retire in panic and confusion from the front as their units/organizations began to suffered reverses and/or severe attrition as a result of the intense combat. These retreating forces—in dribbles at

[41] Betts, "A Revelation of War."

[42] Family history document by Juanita Martin (granddaughter of Eliza Hill). Joanne Baucum, e-mail message to author, August 14, 2007.

first—would not have appeared in significant numbers behind the Federal rear until around 10:00-11:00 A.M.

Then between 11:00 A.M. to 2:30 P.M. the battle still cannot be seen at the cabin. According to Chief Ranger Allen, the closest fighting "is still a considerable distance south, with the Union rally point after 11:30 being in south Jones and nearby Sowell fields, more than a half mile distant and beyond the forested valley of Tilghman Branch. The Federal counterattack at noon relocates the front still further south, advancing the fighting a full mile from Perry Field." By 2:00 P.M. the Union right retreats back to Jones Field, then eventually across Tilghman Branch, to superior defensive ground. At around 2:30 P.M., aides on General Grant‘s staff ride past the old cabin on the Hamburg-Savannah Road and cross Snake Creek to try and find Lew Wallace‘s tardy division.

Between 2:30 P.M. and 4:30 P.M., the cabin would have began to experience some of the battle itself, with the first sighting of "Butternut" uniforms on some, the Rebel flag and taking its first hits with bullet fire. The Union's Sherman has set up a front line at Hamburg-Savannah Road which extended from Russian Tenant Field through Perry Field to Mulberry Field, with McClernand to the south from Mulberry. The soon to be called "Hornet's Nest" is raging further south (one mile) along the Sunken Road. The Confederate advance brings Pond's men across Tilghman Branch but they may have never reached any open fields. Federal blue will bleed blood red upon the same color uniforms of both sides, because many of Pond's Louisiana volunteers, as state-issued militia, were given the same blue colors, therefore receiving fire from their own at times.

Chief Ranger Allen:

This cabin lay on the fringe of battle. No major action

occurs around the structure or the others nearby. This is the reason these buildings survive the battle without suffering any significant or serious damage. After 4 p.m., only long range (quarter mile) exchanges of musketry and cannon fire occur along this sector of the front. The Union position was far too strong for the meager Confederate force in the area to threaten.

Apparently the cabin saw any battle on its front begin to wane between 4:30 P.M. and dark, although firing may have continued at a distance as Confederates have retreated west of Tilghman Branch. The Union line remains at the Russian Tenant Field with Sherman's men along Hamburg-Savannah Road across from Perry and south, engaging other Rebel ranks there with just a long range sporadic firefight at a quarter mile distance.

Chief Ranger Allen:

The location of structures in this area, which includes the old cabin, were just forward—around 75-100 yards—of the main Federal line, but would have been on or either behind the Union skirmish line, maintained on the heights overlooking Tilghman Branch. In fact there is a high probability the three buildings in Perry Field were most likely occupied by Union forces as suitable cover and used as sharpshooter nests.

...the remnant of Buckland's brigade retired into the northern edge of Perry Field on the afternoon of April 6 and at 4:30 P.M., deployed a line of battle (from left to right the 70th Ohio, 48th Ohio, and 72nd Ohio).

In his book *Shiloh, The Battle That Changed the Civil War*, author Larry J. Daniel gives this report, of late in the first days incidents:

The deep, broad ravine of Tilghman Branch ran

parallel to the Tennessee River and extended from Snake Creek to the Western Corinth Road, where it broke into a number of smaller ravines...Although Sherman's and McClernand's divisions managed to keep the Rebels west of the branch, the bluecoats withdrew to defend the Hamburg – Savannah Road and the Snake Creek bridge, thus securing the approach route for Lew Wallace's belated division. Buckland's brigade, the only intact unit remaining with Sherman, came into line along the northern portion of the James Perry Field. Although the fences along the road had been torn down, blackberry and sassafras bushes still marked the border of the open field (a cotton field, Sherman later recalled) in their front.

Sherman had dispatched Captain J. H. Hammond to the landing to summon additional artillery. About 3:30, the six guns of Captain Edward Bouton's Battery I, 1st Illinois Light Artillery, rumbled into northern Perry Field. Arriving with the Chicago gunners were 250 men of the 53rd Ohio, about all that remained of Hildebrand's brigade, which was placed in support of the battery.

Between Perry and Mulberry fields was a densely wooded ravine that extended two hundred yards. Sherman feared that it might be occupied by enemy snipers in an effort to drive off the artillerymen...

About 4:00, Bouton's battery was shelled from the south end of Perry Field across Tilghman Branch. A lengthy and brutal exchange erupted with Ketchum's Alabama Battery, later reinforced with the Washington Artillery, which the Chicago press labeled the "Great Artillery Duel." Although having one gun and a number of horses disabled, Bouton maintained his position until 5:00 [P.M.].[43]

Captain William H. Ketchum, Alabama Battery, reports this in his '*Official Record:*'

[43] Larry J. Daniel, *Shiloh: The Battle that Changed the Civil War* (New York: Touchstone/Simon & Shuster, 1997), 238-239.

This same evening we engaged one of the enemy's batteries and silenced it after about half an hour's firing. Night coming on, we placed our pieces in battery on their parade ground, adjoining a house on the right of their camp, where a number of our dead and wounded lay. This was at the instance of Colonel Ferguson, of General Beauregard's staff. On our left in the woods was our infantry support, Colonel Pond's command.[44]

Snake Creek Bridge[45]

Darkness brings an end to the immediate conflict with positions above held as indicated for the night around Perry Field. It appears the old cabin is in a no-man's-land for the night. However, it will witness from the north the late arrival of

[44] War Department, *Official Records*, 528.

[45] U. S. Grant, "The Battle of Shiloh," *The Century Magazine*, Vol. XXIX, No. 4, (Feb., 1885), http://cdl.library.cornell.edu/cgi-bin/moa/sgml/moa-idx?notisid=ABP2287-0029-136, 598.

Lew Wallace's reinforcement division across Snake Creek Bridge about nightfall. This is "the same bridge he understood had been submerged only three days before."[46] It is the same bridge the census taker came across in 1850 to find first, the Wickers at the cabin now to become part of history. The bridge was "reconstructed" by the Union, according to *'OR'* reports, after being initially submerged by flooding upon their arrival at Pittsburg Landing.[47] Once across it, Wallace says in his *'OR'* report: "About 1 o'clock at night my brigades and batteries were disposed, forming the extreme right, and ready for battle."[48]

Chief Ranger Allen:

Buckland's troops formed Sherman's right flank in support of Bouton's battery. When Lew Wallace's troops arrived, Smith's brigade deployed in advance of Buckland and bivouacked for the night. Two of Buckland's regiments (70th and 72nd Ohio) spent the night in line of battle at this location, while the 48th Ohio went to Pittsburg Landing...

Sounds will continue into the night; some of battle, some of nature. Union gunboats will fire the night through, trying to hit the spirit of the Rebels, if not their bodies. That sounding boom is no respecter of persons, however, and will awaken and disturb men of both sides. It will be soon joined by nature's own cannon fire, as thunder and lightning from a spring storm blazons the battlefield and roars down about midnight. At least it all helps deafen the moans and cries from the wounded on both sides, whether in camp within tents or shelter, or, still strewn about the battlefield, their cries for help

---

[46] Steven E. Woodworth, ed., *Grant's Lieutenant's from Cairo to Vicksburg*, "'*If He Had Less Rank*,' Lewis Wallace," Stacy D. Allen, (Lawrence, KS: University Press of Kansas, 2001), 76.

[47] War Department, *Official Records*, 181.

[48] War Department, *Official Records*, 170.

seemingly falling on deaf ears, the rain from storm at least filling thirsty mouths, quenching their particular cry for water. Perhaps prayers answered from a higher authority than man.

Reports are that hogs from farms in the battle areas, either loosed by battle or by hunger brought on by owners long vacated from the field, are heard in the night and shown by lightning, already feeding upon the dead, probably man and horse alike. It depicts a level of life at that point.

Who slept in "Wicker Cabin" on Perry Field that night? Was it no one if in a no-man's-land as stated? Or, was it used to house wounded, either of their own volition, or, that of either side intentionally? Did officers seek its refuge over others of less rank? If any suggested were so, did they utilize any comforts left behind by now vacated private citizens, at the very least escaping earlier to save their own lives? Or perhaps it just lay vacant, providing shelter to no one for the night.

One possible answer is seen in the '*OR*' report of Lt. Col. Manning F. Force of the Twentieth Ohio Infantry, part of Wallace's arrivals. With this author's bracket insert and underlining, Force states:

> *The Twentieth Ohio, under my command (Colonel Whittlesey commanding the brigade), arrived after dark from Adamsville at the camp of the Fifty-first Ohio, near Pittsburg Landing. It was posted for the night on the northern slope of a ravine [Tilghman Ravine], and there lay on their arms in line of battle till morning...Company D, Captain McElroy, <u>was stationed in a log house outside of the extreme right</u> and the other companies drawn in line in a slight hollow.*[49]

Sounds like a good possibility to be the old cabin, or one of them on Perry Field. Another reference to a "log-house" is found in General Grant's memoirs. He states the following

[49] War Department, *Official Records*, 201.

about Sunday night of the battle, with this author's underlining:

The right of my line rested near the bank of Snake Creek, a short distance above the bridge which had been built [reconstructed] by the troops for the purpose of connecting Crump's landing and Pittsburg landing.

Sherman had posted some troops in a log-house and out-buildings which overlooked both the bridge over which Wallace was expected and the creek above that point. In this last position Sherman was frequently attacked before night, but held the point until he voluntarily abandoned it to advance in order to make room for Lew Wallace, who came up after dark.[50]

Was this also a reference to cabin's on Perry Field? Or was it further to the north where buildings were on the Russian Tenant Field? More speculation for sure but at the very least, "happenings" that occurred around or close to the old cabin. The bridge was already in existence from at least since before the 1850 census as already reported. However, also as previously indicated, it was reconstructed. There's more of the full report in this *'OR'* from Major General James B. McPherson, who was at the time of Shiloh, a Lt. Colonel and "chief of engineers," as reported by Lt. Col. John A. Rawlins, Assistant Adjutant-General in his *'OR'* report on Wallace's arrival. McPherson reports:

When the troops first disembarked at Pittsburgh Landing the Tennessee River was very high, the water backing up in all the streams, covering the bottoms in the vicinity of the river from 2 to 6 feet, rendering the Lick and Snake Creek's impassable...As soon as the water subsided sufficiently the

---

[50] Ulysses S. Grant, *Personal Memoirs of U. S. Grant* (1885), The Project Gutenberg EBook of Personal Memoirs of U. S. Grant, Complete, June 2004, http://www.gutenberg.org/files/4367/4367-h/4367-h.htm.

bridge across the creek [Snake Creek] was reconstructed and a company of cavalry went through to communicate with General [Lew] Wallace's command. This was on Thursday, previous to the battle.[51]

The Second Day of the Battle for the Old Cabin…

For the old cabin, the second day of the battle brought a rush of Federal blue across Perry Field, by Lew Wallace's men at 8:00 A.M. and then Sherman's men at 10:00 A.M. They crossed Tilghman Branch to take up the fight anew, buoying the Union cause, with Wallace's reinforcements (and Buell's by boat, elsewhere). Artillery was set up on the field by the Union's Thompson, with Bouton to their left. They shelled Ketchum's Confederate guns a quarter mile to the west across the ravine, who again returned the fire, with subsequent duel fierce bombardment taking place. Chief Ranger Allen stated, at that time, Smith's brigade, who was Wallace's left, was on Perry Field as was Buckland's.

Chief Ranger Allen:

The next morning, Buckland advanced with the rest of Sherman's command into Jones Field, where Wallace's division, who had preceded them (by two hours) were engaged with the Confederate left. There, at 10 A.M., Buckland moved southward to the center of the field, taking a position midway in the field, where his force engaged Confederate troops deployed in the forest located south and west of the field.

Wallace's report of that morning from his '*OR*':

Shortly after daybreak Captain Thompson opened fire on a rebel battery posted on a bluff opposite my First Brigade,

[51] War Department, *Official Records*, 181.

and across a deep and prolonged hollow, threaded by a creek and densely wooded on both sides. From its position and that of its infantry support, lining the whole length of the bluff, it was apparent that crossing the hollow would be at heavy loss, unless the battery was first driven off. Thurber was accordingly posted to assist Thompson by a cross-fire and at the same time sweep the hiding place of the rebels on the brow of the hill. This had the desired effect. After a few shells from Thurber the enemy fell back, but not before Thompson had dismounted one of their rifled guns.[52]

In Cunningham's *Shiloh and the Western Campaign of 1862* he says of Wallace 2nd day:

...heavy fighting raged on the extreme Confederate left, or Union right, as Lew Wallace's third division finally went into battle...Confederate forces in front of Wallace's unit were comparatively weak, consisting of parts of Ponds brigade, fragments of a couple of Tennessee regiments, and a section of artillery belonging to Ketchum's Battery. When Wallace's men first advance that morning the two guns were ordered forward to support the Confederate infantry. Wallace's Ninth Indiana Battery, Captain Noah Thompson commanding, opened first fire on the Southern gunners. The two Confederate guns, brought into action despite the Union fire, were soon busy dropping rounds into the enemy's ranks. The Indiana gunners averaged almost two hundred rounds per gun on Monday, a good portion of them fired at Ketchum's guns; but most of them either over shot or fell short.

A 6-pound ball did bowl over one of the Alabama gunners, but he was the only casualty for over an hour.[53]

---

[52] War Department, *Official Records*, 170.

[53] O. Edward Cunningham, *Shiloh and the Western Campaign of 1862*, Gary D. Joiner and Timothy B. Smith, eds., (New York, NY: Savas Beatie LLC, 2007), 363.

There were other '*Official Record*' reports of the morning:

First, under Sherman and Buckland's commands, is that of Lieut. Col. Job R. Parker, Forty-eighth Ohio Infantry, "On the morning of the 7th we were called upon to support a battery upon our right wing. Here we remained until the opposing battery was silenced, when we were again brought into a hot action with rebel infantry…"[54]

Under same commands is Col. Joseph R. Cockerill, Seventieth Ohio Infantry, "Early in the morning of the 7th a severe cannonade was opened by General Wallace's battery on our right, and we were ordered to advance, which we did in good order, the Forty-eighth on the right, Seventieth in the center, and Seventy-second on the left."[55]

From the Confederate side under Pond's command, Capt. Ketchum reports:

Daylight in the morning found our teams hitched up, our men chilled through by the cold rain, sleeping without tents or much covering; still, most manfully and cheerfully did they man their pieces to reply to a battery which opened on us. In this position we fought them half an hour, and finding they had our range, and our situation too much exposed, losing some of our horses, I retired about 100 yards to a position which I desired the evening previous.[56]

Shiloh Park online web site reports:

April 7: The battle resumed early with an artillery duel between Lew Wallace's field artillery (i.e., Thurber's Missouri and Thompson's Indiana batteries, supported by Bouton's unassigned Illinois battery) and Ketchum's Alabama Battery

---

[54] War Department, *Official Records*, 270.
[55] War Department, *Official Records*, 271.
[56] War Department, *Official Records*, 528.

deployed on the north edge of Jones field near Colonel Hare's abandoned brigade headquarters. When ordered forward (south: parallel and astride the route of Highway 22), Wallace's division advanced across the broad valley of Tilghman Branch at 6:30 a.m. For the next hour the stronger Union division steadily forced Pond's infantry and Ketchum's battery to retire southward. After securing the northern end of Jones field, Wallace held his ground astride this tract and waited for the...arrival of Sherman's command. That Federal force was expected to advance west across the Tilghman valley to connect with...Wallace's left.[57]

Of the morning, Wiley Sword, in *Shiloh: Bloody April*, reports:

At daylight one of his [Lew Wallace's] battery commanders, Captain Noah S. Thompson of the 9th Indiana Battery, discovered Ketchum's Alabama Battery in park amid some of McClernand's camps in Jones field.

The range was about four hundred yards, and Thompson suddenly opened fire, catching the Alabamans unaware. Yet Ketchum's gunners jumped up to man their pieces, and for a half-hour the reverberations of cannon fire filled the air.

Wallace was alert to the opportunities afforded by the topography and brought up Thurber's Missouri Battery toward his right. Added to the rain of shells falling on the Confederates, Thurber's fire placed their guns at a further disadvantage...

By now Ketchum's gunners were beginning to reel under the heavy shelling. Their guns were exposed to a cross fire, and some of their best horses had been killed. Limbering up his cannon, Ketchum retired about one hundred yards to a

[57] Shiloh National Military Park, Tennessee – Mississippi, "Park Administration and History, Land Protection Plan," (2002 Biennial Review), http://www.nps.gov/archive/shil/admlpp.htm.

position affording better cover.

Having witnessed the departure of the enemy artillery from the bluff, Wallace quickly sent his five thousand troops forward. Soon his brigades emerged in echelon, with a long line of skirmishers covering their front.

Then Sword stated though, "For a while it appeared they would be little fighting at all. Having advanced to the bluff overlooking Tilghman Creek, Lew Wallace ordered his men to halt until Sherman…advanced to…support."[58]

Either the old cabin was out of range of both the artillery barrages (one of Sunday evening, the other the next morning), or it was cradled within the arms of both day's fate, as it was not destroyed. Perhaps it was scarred both days from bullets intended, or, gone astray. It had survived and would remain and become part of not only the military history there but a private one as well.

A fictional story (but based on actual facts) that unfolded near the cabin premises was written in the novel, *Shiloh*, by famed Civil War author Shelby Foote. In his chapter called "Squad," he depicts the above by way of a soldier's experience at the beginning of the day. In presenting a soldier as part of Lew Wallace's division in the 23rd Indiana Infantry that had arrived across Snake Creek Bridge the night before, Foote writes in the soldier's words (with this author's added bracket inserts):

Our division, Lew Wallace commanding, was in position on the side of a hollow. There were thick woods on both sides and a creek down in the draw [Tilghman Branch]. Across it, half a mile away, where the opposite slope rose up in a bluff, the rebels were lined up waiting. We could see their battle flags and sunlight sparkling on a battery [Ketchum's]

[58] Sword, 384, 406.

near the center of their line.

We were the flank division of Grants army. Snake Creek, which we crossed the night before, was off to our right. When dawn broke and the sun came through the haze, I lay there in the grass, watching it glint on the field pieces, and I thought: Oh-oh. If Wallace sends us across that hollow in the face of those guns, he's going to have considerably fewer of us when we reach the other side.

There was a long quiet period, nearly an hour, while the two armies lay and looked across the vacant space like two dogs sizing each other up. And firing began to sputter over on the left, like growling, nothing much it first but finally a steady clatter, growing louder..., swelling along the front toward where we lay...

...I really thought our time had come. But Wallace had more sense than to send us naked across that draw against those guns. He ordered up two of his batteries, one in front of where we were [Thompson] and another down the line [Bouton]. They tuned up, ranging in on the brassy glints on the bluff. We enjoyed watching them work. Thompson's battery, which was directly to our front, did especially well. We watched the balls rise like black dots, getting smaller, then come down on the rebel guns across the hollow. The cannoneers were lively, proud to be putting on a show, and every now and then we cheered them. It didn't last long. As soon as one of the secesh ['secessionist'] guns was dismounted by a direct hit, the whole battery limbered and got out. That was what we had been waiting for.

It's not often you see the war the way a civilian thinks it is, that it was that way now. We were center brigade, and since our company - G - was just to the right of the brigade center, we saw the whole show....When the rebel batteries fell back, their infantry went with it.[59]

Then, still another view from the Rebel side can be seen as reported in *Eyewitnesses at the Battle of Shiloh*, compiled and edited by David R. Logsden. In it he states, "Lew Wallace's Union Division, moving southwest from the Hamburg-Savannah Road, surprises Pond's regiments, camped at the extreme left of the Confederate line." One of the 'eyewitness' reports is from a Lt. Grisamore, 18th Louisiana, Pond's Brigade:

We were...put into a line at...the top of the location in front of the ravine in which we had encamped. Simultaneous with this movement, the skirmishers of the enemy appeared in the ravine before us...We fired upon them, driving them back, but in a few minutes a battery which was in position about 300 or 400 yards in front opened on us, sending their shot through the trees over our heads. We were ordered to fall back.[60]

And so the 2nd day continues. From 10:00 A.M. until noon, the battle at its western end moves across the ravine back to Jones Field and beyond. The Southern cause is struck and retreat is the new order of the day for them. By 3 P.M. the cabin will have only heard and seen repetitively what it did the day before, except in reverse. The battle is down to Hamburg-Purdy Road. As Chief Ranger Allen states, "All principle combat occurs west of Tilghman Branch, and after 10 A.M., moves southward. Once Wallace seizes the northern end of Jones Field, Perry Field is no longer of concern as to what transpires for the remainder of the battle."

After 3 P.M. until dark the battle winds down with one

---

[59] Shelby Foote, *Shiloh*, 1991 ed. (New York: Vintage/Random House, 1952), 165-167.

[60] David R. Logsdon, ed. *Eyewitnesses at the Battle of Shiloh*, (Nashville, TN: Kettle Mills Press, 1994), 70.

final charge by the Rebels from Shiloh Church at 4 P.M., checking the Union advance. It allows the "Rebs" full retreat and the Federal forces follow only until about a half mile south of Shiloh Branch, then retreat themselves to the battlefield.

Chief Ranger Allen then reports on the following day:

On April 8, two Federal divisions (T.J. Wood and Sherman) advance south by southwest off the battlefield. The force advancing on the right, elements from Sherman's battered division engage Confederate cavalry at an area known as Fallen Timbers, roughly six road miles southwest of Pittsburg Landing (three air miles southwest of Shiloh church), on the Ridge or Bark road. Confederate forces retreat and Sherman captures a Confederate field hospital, sending his cavalry another mile westward where they encounter the strong enemy rearguard near Mickey's (current day Pebble Hill community). All evidence illustrates to Sherman the Confederates are in a full retreat and no longer pose an immediate threat to the Union army, and pursuant to his orders, he retires his force to his original camps.

The Battle of Shiloh is now history and thus ends this author's use of the above military input and references of Chief Park Ranger Stacy Allen.

Charles Shedd, in his park history said this of Shiloh: "…in a few days only the debris of the battle and the graves of the dead were left to tell of the bloody struggle which had made the name of a little country chapel one of the most tragic in American history."[61]

James Lee McDonough, said in his preface of, *Shiloh – in Hell before Night*, "The battle is fascinating too because of the human interest stories associated with it. Some of the most unusual, pathetic, and heartrending occurrences conceivable

[61] Shedd, "A History of Shiloh National Military Park Tennessee."

took place there."[62]

Some are told by Gaye Granger Stokes in the Bell history (soon to be old cabin related):

Sarah's homestead was located on the west side of the Tennessee River in an area known then as Pittsburg Landing. Her cabins were right across the road from the place where the future Confederate General Albert Sidney Johnston would bleed to death from the wound received in the battle at Shiloh.

During this battle, Sarah's cabins were destroyed and her cotton field and peach orchard were the scene of some of the fiercest fighting to take place in the battle. It was said that toward the end of the first day the cotton field was so thick with bodies that one couldn't get across it without stepping from body to body. The peach trees were in bloom and the minie balls were so thick that the blossoms were cut to pieces and fell to the ground like snowflakes.

My grandmother, Mayme Hamilton Bell, used to tell me stories of the pond that was red with the blood of wounded and dying soldiers - North and South.

Others told of the wounded horses that also sought out the water of that "Bloody Pond" which is what it has been known as ever since. The pond is right next to Sarah's peach orchard. Sarah never rebuilt her cabins after the battle.[63]

Sarah Bell's failure to have her cabin rebuilt will later prove true by the census of 1870 when she is still living there on her property but with the Georges in the now moved 'Wicker' cabin. Further detail of that will be reported in covering the 1870 census. Because of the intense fighting on all the Bell property and others in the vicinity on both days of

[62] James Lee McDonough, *Shiloh – in Hell before Night*, (Knoxville: The University of Tennessee Press, 1977), Preface.
[63] Stokes, "The Bell Family at Shiloh."

the battle, not only was Sarah Bell's cabin destroyed but Manse George's original one was as well. It is detailed in some historical references as being used by both sides at given battlefield control times, even indicating an enemy flag raised from it.[64]

Like a hail of bullets, rain on Bloody Pond, still cleansing soldier's blood. Author's photo.

[64] Sword, 321.

Chapter 6:
The Cabin After The Battle

Obviously, any rightful occupants of the cabin were not to return for some time, if at all. So who spent Monday night of April 7, 1862, in the cabin? Did anyone? Did the Union side respect any of its remaining contents and forbid anyone being there? Or, was it again, inhabited by the wounded, or officers seeking a headquarters or anyone for the night? These questions remain unanswered and probably will, allowing speculation.

A few weeks after the battle in 1862, William Manse George (neighbor in 1860 to Lewis Wicker), whose cabin was probably completely destroyed, apparently bought a battle-surviving cabin which was on Perry Field. It can be debated, *ad infinitum* (to infinity), as to whom he bought it from, and, from where he moved it. Was it from James Perry on his field or Widow Flora Wicker (per her family and others) from Perry or Wicker Fields? The best conclusion is that Mr. George moved it from what is known today as Perry Field, near the park entrance, to its present location today, next to the Peach Orchard.

Sometime during the two day battle, Flora's cabin and the other four (+) family ones on or near Wicker Field, would have been destroyed. However, she had hers rebuilt. Since Flora's son Alvis did not join his military unit until six months after Shiloh, he may have rebuilt hers during that time. Whatever involvement, if any, she and Alvis had in the moved cabin is unknown for sure.

What took place in order for Manse George to decide to buy and move what would now be a vacated old Wicker cabin on Perry Field? Who was in it prior to battle time and who sold it afterwards? Speculation can abound. It appears someone didn't return to it after the battle, at least to continue to live in it, so one would assume it sat empty at a given point. James A. Perry would be the leading candidate to sell it but he may have been deceased by then also, perhaps even from Shiloh. His son, J. A. J. Perry, lived close by in 1860 as did Alvis Wicker as mentioned. At any rate, Mr. George bought it from someone.

How did he move the cabin? The first thought was he pulled it by mule or oxen team, rolling it on poles, replaced from the back to the front as it moved. However, the consensus of opinion is that it was disassembled, and possibly marked, to reassemble on site. One story, as part of the Bell family at Shiloh history, recounts how Miriam Bell Holden, in her nineties today, "remembers hearing the story from her mother's family of her great grandfather Jones hauling all the logs for the George cabin to its present site."[65]

Although initially this author had not been able to talk personally to Miriam (Bell) Holden, research determined who her Jones ancestor was by full name. There was enough information to collect from the aforementioned Bell/Hargrove/George family histories, together with running out names on various censuses to determine who he was. Her great grandfather (on her mother's sides) was Perry Clark Jones, neighbor to the Georges and Sarah Bell in 1870. She had sold land to Jones that he lived on. This is conveyed now as he will come into play later in the old cabin's, and, the park's history.

The Bell history says the cabin came from nearby Wicker Field, not Perry Field. That basis is a letter received by

[65] Stokes.

a Manse George (Nancy Bell married Manse George) family member in 1985 from George Reaves, Chief, Interpretation and Resources Management at Shiloh National Military Park. In it he states, "The Manse George Cabin was moved to its present location from Wicker Field about two weeks after the battle."

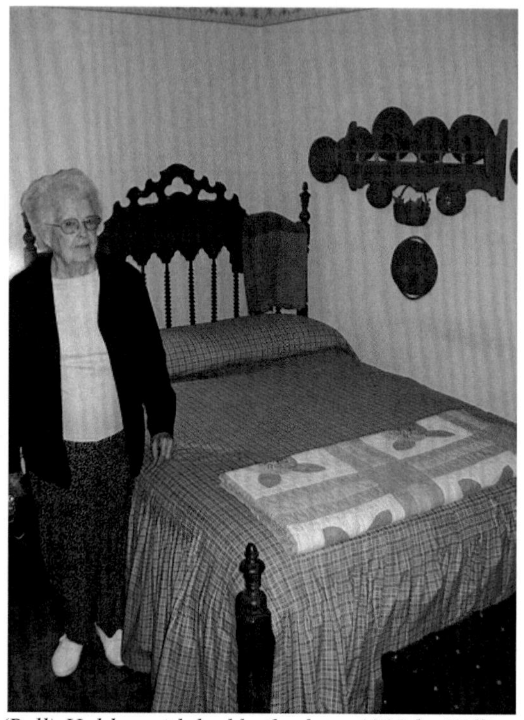

Miriam (Bell) Holden with bed built about 1830 by William Strawn. Author's photo.

Although this can be entertained, and even possible (if any cabins survived there?), as maybe the Wickers brought it with them to Wicker Field from Perry Field in or after 1853. Was it moved twice? It is possible but probably not in this author's opinion. This is because two older documents, already presented, indicate it came from what is now known as Perry Field. One is the booklet *Shiloh*, mentioned previously, written by a park historian, Albert Dillahunty, in the 1950's. The other being the research paper from 1934 that accurately depicted the following, with author Duane Helweg's bracketed inserts:

But several years before the War Between the States [November 6, 1848], Louis [sic-'Lewis'] Wicker had bought land [400 acres in Entry #1723] in the Pittsburg area and had built a house near the place on which the Tilghman home was located later [deeds show at today's park entrance, running north]. This dwelling stood through the battle, and sometime after the conflict, Manse George purchased it, and moved it to the site which his former residence occupied, thus building what in future years was to be known as the "War Cabin." With the exception of a few logs which have replaced old ones because of decay all of the logs in this house are the battle scarred ones of the Louis [sic-'Lewis'] Wicker home.[66]

Another letter from Superintendent Zeb McKinney of the park in 1988 to a Bell family member, simply calls the Manse George Cabin, "the oldest building on the battlefield." It was a replacement for their original home which was destroyed during the battle.

With regard to Ranger Reaves reference to a "Wicker Field" move for the cabin, and in deference to what he knew, it may simply be the confusion that existed for this author originally over where Lewis Wicker owned land (1848-1853), on and north of today's Perry Field, and where he ended up a tenant, on today's Wicker Field (1854-1860+), south and over a mile apart. Nonetheless, it is ironic to have the old cabin follow the Wicker's to just past Bloody Pond, by the Peach Orchard and adjacent to Wicker Field.

Author's note: George A. Reaves became involved enough and respected enough during his tenure at Shiloh that

[66] Durbin, "The War Cabin."

he was allowed to be buried in Shiloh Church Cemetery, although not a church family member. Mr. Reaves also co-authored a book about Shiloh:

Joseph Allen Frank and George A. Reaves, "Seeing the Elephant" Raw Recruits at the Battle of Shiloh (Urbana and Chicago: University of Illinois Press, 2003).

Following is Reaves grave picture:

George Reaves grave at Shiloh Church Cemetery. Author's photo.

Recovery after the War

Families suffered the loss of their homes in the battle due either to burning, bullets or cannon fire or all three. One thinks of the loss of life and limb in the course of the battle but for those soldiers who survived, they still had homes to go to, somewhere, while the Shiloh locals had none, save family or friends to the north or south. Wherever the survivor's were, hearts would have been heavy, certainly over the loss of their homes, but more importantly, over the loss of sons, husbands and fathers. By the 1870 census a war-orphaned granddaughter was still living with her grandmother, Flora Wicker, as neighbors to the George's who were now in the old cabin, relocated to its present site. Perhaps these tragedies were still reminders of the battle, as the following poem depicts:

If you stand soft and silent
In the night's early chill,
You can still hear the cannon
Roar across "Shiloh Hill."
-Mark Putnam[67]

Recovery was still possible, however, as life goes on. Homes were rebuilt, livestock reacquired, fields replanted. Even wild game would return to the woods, with flora slowly growing back, even overgrowing the signs of what had occurred those two historical days in and around Shiloh Church. The Sunken Road, location of the infamous "Hornet's Nest," where Confederate cannons tore the trees to shreds, today lies behind and within sight of the old cabin and has regrowth along it.

Part of Sunken Road lies in the woods behind the cabin. Author's photo.

[67] Shiloh National Military Park, Tennessee – Mississippi, "Park Administration and History, Land Protection Plan."

What was home life like for those private citizens whose dwellings either survived or were repaired or rebuilt after the battle? About 1875, the Reverend Thomas Cotton, former Union chaplain, was invited to a Shiloh Church meeting where he was promised a "bush arbor" would be built.[68] Below is an example of such a structure, or "brush" arbor:

Brush Arbor[69]

In Rev. Cotton's 1899 typewritten work, entitled "The Cross and the Flag," which chronicles his thirty years of ministry; he tells a story about an historian who encountered a Shiloh local. In April 1866, the Shiloh Battlefield was visited by famous pictorial historian, Benson J. Lossing. In his work on the American Civil War, he told of meeting a Mrs. Sowell and being invited to take supper and lodging. Although almost

[68] Rev. Thomas Cotton, "The Cross and the Flag," 1899 typewritten work, courtesy of Larry DeBerry.
[69] Harris Chapel Holiness Ch., "Old Brush Arbor Days," www.harrischapelholinesschurch.org/history.htm.

exactly four years after the battle, one finds his descriptions most appropriate to describe potential life in the old Wicker cabin, now occupied by the Georges. In fact, Dr. Lossing may well have observed the cabin while there, as follows:

...We were, as we soon ascertained, at the parting of the ways for Hamburg and Pittsburg Landings. While deliberating which to take, and considering seriously where we might obtain supper and lodging, for the gloom of twilight was gathering in the woods, the questions were settled by a woman (Mrs. Sowell) on a gaunt gray horse, with her little boy, about six years of age, striding the animal's back behind her. She kindly consented to give us such entertainment as she could. "It is but little I have," she said, in a pleasant, plaintive voice, and we expressed our willingness to be content therewith. So we followed her through the woods and a few open fields for nearly a mile in the direction of Pittsburg Landing, and at dark were at her home, not far from McClernand's camp on Sunday morning, where the battle raged with so much fury. All around it were the marks of war in scarred, decapitated, and shattered trees, and the remains of clothing and accouterments strewing the ground.

Our hostess was a widow, with six children. Her husband was dying with consumption [tuberculosis] when the battle commenced. <u>She did not leave him, but remained in the house with her children throughout that terrible storm of war</u>. A heavy shell went through her house, and several trees standing near it were cut off or shattered by them. "The Lord was with me," she piously said, as we sat at her humble table, lighted by a lamp composed of wick and melted lard in a tin dish, and supping upon hoe-cake without butter, just baked in the ashes, some fried bacon, and coffee without milk or sugar. "My husband died, but my children were spared," she said; "but God only knows what will become of them in this desolated country, without a school or a church."

Pictorial of Mrs. Sowell on horseback with young son astride behind

We had just come in from the enjoyment of the bright moonlight, and balmy April air, and the burden of the whippowil [sic], and felt that peace and serenity imparted by nature in repose, that inclines one to forgive as we hope to be forgiven. The sweet spell was broken when, in that dingy and battered cabin, lighted by a few blazing fagots and the primitive lamp, with only one half-bottomed chair and a rude box or two to sit upon, we looked upon that lonely, suffering, educated woman, with her six really pretty and intelligent boys and girls, half clad, but clean, struggling for the right to live an example of like misery in thousands of households, once prosperous and happy, thus crushed into poverty by the wickedness of a few ambitious men. In that presence, the Rebellion seemed doubly infernal, and the spirit of forgiveness departed.

We slept soundly in one of the log houses, with our horse stabled in an adjoining room, nailed up for the night, to keep him from the clutches of prowling bushwhackers, and the pigs grunting under our open floor; and at dawn we went out, while the cuckoo's song was sweetest and the mocking-bird's varied carols were loudest, and rambled far over the battle-field, meeting here a tree cut down by shot near its base, there a huge one split by a shell that passed through it and plunged deeply into another beyond, and everywhere little hillocks covering the remains of the slain.

OUR LODGING-PLACE ON THE FIELD OF SHILOH.

Pictorial of Mrs. Sowell's home at Shiloh in April, 1866

After an early breakfast we rode to Pittsburg Landing...and then, riding along the greater portion of the lines of battle from Lick Creek to Owl Creek, we visited the site of Shiloh Meeting-house...and again striking the Corinth road at the ruins of widow Rey's [sic – 'Rea'] house, returned to that village by way of Farmington, where Paine and Marmaduke had a skirmish, in time to take the afternoon train to the scene of another battle, Iuka Springs, twenty miles eastward. [70]

In checking census records for both 1860 and 1870, the young boy described by Dr. Lossing, on horseback behind his mother, Widow Sowell (with six kids in 1870), would have

[70] Benson J. Lossing, *Pictorial History of the Civil War in the United States of America* (Hartford: T. Belknap, Publisher, 1868), Internet Archive, http://www.archive.org/details/pictorialhistory02loss.

been James White Sowell. He, ironically, would become the grandfather of Miriam (Bell) Holden, mentioned previously, and, he would also become a park employee someday and undoubtedly had occasion to work at or at least visit the old cabin. Lossing's story, conveyed by Mrs. Sowell, instills the idea that at least some private citizens remained and survived on the battlefield along with their homes, particularly on the fringes, as did the old cabin on nearby Perry Field.

Further post-war impact upon the local "cabin-living" citizens can be seen from the following excerpts. The first is from B. G. Brazelton's 1885 Hardin County history:

From the Shiloh battle until the close of the Rebellion the citizens were disturbed but very little by regular troops, but armed bands that shunned the regular army created confusion now and then.

The river being protected by gunboats enabled the needy citizens to procure supplies from the North until the war was over. In order to get what he wanted, a man had to prove to the Federal authorities that he had been loyal to the United States during the war. Before this the people had to manufacture their own clothing as best they could, and use wheat in the place of coffee.

In the spring of 1865 the news of Gen. Lee's surrender to Gen. Grant on the 6th of April was received. The people knew now that the Rebellion was about over and of course there was some rejoicing. It was not long until peace was proclaimed, and the soldiers that had escaped death began to return home to leave no more for the battle-field...The county now presented a different appearance to what it did in 1860; in fact, it almost seemed like a new county. The four years of war had caused small game to become plentiful; even the deer and turkey, that were scarcely seen before the war, were numerous in places. The catamount [cougar] screamed occasionally, and the black bear was to be seen now and then. As soon as it was known that a man could hunt without being molested, the hollow trees were robbed of their old rusty guns [hidden from the Union], and then there was such a killing of game as had not been known since the first settling of the county.

Notwithstanding, the people seemed rejoiced at the news of peace, the war had left a stain that a century could not remove...Common schools had nearly been forgotten, and many a child had grown up without even the knowledge of a school-house...During that dreadful time it was a common thing to see the ladies filling the places of their husbands or brothers at the plow-handles. But few owned a horse, and most of the plowing was done with oxen... Most of the church, school, and gin-houses were burnt long before the close of the war, but it was not long after peace was made until improvements began rapidly.

Man plowing with an ox[71]

The news of peace was received by the people as joyful tidings...But it was a hard matter to rejoice much or

[71] "Department of Conservation Photograph Collection, 1937-1976," *Tennessee Virtual Archive (TeVA).*

long at a time, for much of the sad effect of war was still visible, especially to the farmers. Instead of wealth amid prosperity existing as before the war, the county bore a sad appearance. The farms that in 1860 looked beautiful and full of life were now much overgrown with bushes and briers, and, of course, looked desolate to the spectator who viewed them, before the Rebellion. The fencing was much decayed, torn down, and in many places had been burned up by passing armies.

As soon as the civil law was declared in force, lawsuits began between citizens for property taken, and for other damages done, during the war. These suits lasted only a few years, and are now nearly forgotten, as they should be, by citizens living in the same county, and working for their own good, and desiring the happiness and the friendship of others around them.[72]

The second post-war excerpt is from the Charles Shedd park history from 1954, where he references the following from Miss "Lera" Durbin:

With the end of the war, the inhabitants set about to rebuild their ruined fortunes with the same determination which had settled the wilderness and carved homes from it. The small farmers of Hardin County, with their tradition of self-reliance, were quick to rebuild. Within a few years most of the physical scars wrought by the war had disappeared. However, the bitter feuds engendered by the war still divided the county, and violence was common in the decade following the end of hostilities. One witness to those troubled times recalled, years later, that a citizen living on the Shiloh battlefield was murdered by a band of marauders after the war had ended. By the end of the Reconstruction period [1877], Hardin County

[72] Brazelton, *A History of Hardin County*.

had settled once more into its traditional rural way of life.[73]

[73] Lera Durbin, "Five Years of War" in ms. History of Hardin County, Shiloh NMP, 1934, p. 2, quoted in Charles E. Shedd, Jr., Park Historian, "A History of Shiloh National Military Park Tennessee."

Chapter 7:
The 1870 Census...
Family Connections
To The Cabin Continue

In 1870, Mansefield George and Nancy are still living in the Wicker family's old moved cabin. Daughter Sarah is age 15 (born October 26, 1853),[74] Mary is 11 and son William is six, having been born in the old cabin after Manse moved it. Some of the Bell family was still near the peach orchard, but Widow Sarah was now living with the George's, although the census enumerator failed to show her last name as Bell. Initially it was thought she was his mother until this was read in the Bell history. "In the 1870 Census she lived with her daughter and son-in-law, Nancy and Manse George, in the cabin that was moved to the corner of the peach orchard for them after the War [sic-'battle']."[75]

They were all now living in what would eventually be called the "War Cabin" by the War Department. McCuller's and Hargrove's were also still nearby in this census. Robert Hargrove, age 23 (born April 26, 1846),[76] will come-a-courtin' to the cabin and marry Sarah George shortly after this census

---

[74] Sevier County Arkansas, "Lockesburg Cemetery," (ARGENWEB), http://www.genealogyshoppe.com/arsevier/lockescem.htm.
[75] Stokes, "The Bell Family at Shiloh."
[76] Sevier County Arkansas, "Lockesburg Cemetery."

as their first child, Molly, was born before 1872, perhaps even in the cabin, if relatives Nancy George and Sarah Bell mid-wifed in it.

Next door in the 1870 census, the "Widow Wicker," or Flora, was living with teenage granddaughter Susan Wicker (orphan of Matthew) and a Thomas Wicker (family connection unknown). Elzina and husband D. B. Green with their children are in a cabin there and they were all on what is now known in the park as Wicker Field. Neighbor's Wicker, Green and George offspring no doubt played together in or around the old moved cabin. At times, the older girls may have even tended Elzina's younger children in either home.

How long did it take for what was now referred to as "Bloody Pond" between the Georges and Bells, Wickers and Greens, to become useable water again? Stained red by the blood of wounded soldiers and horses, from both sides, who had walked or dragged themselves there to drink, only to quench their fiery thirst for the last time before life's breath left their bodies bleeding as openly as the pond's surface itself. No doubt daily reminders were still around in 1870, and farming practices may have uncovered them for years to come; buttons, bullets and bones. The dead were buried everywhere, some in shallow graves, eventually exposed by the elements or animals.

Names like Fraley, Howell, Hagy, Sowell, House, Davis, Pickens and Jones were also still around the cabin. To the north were more Wickers; Alvis was still apparently on Perry Field. Next door were his sister Sarah and husband William, the Edwards having not rebuilt on or near Wicker Field. The Perry's are gone, thus providing the possibility of Sarah living in the other remaining cabin of the potential three the Wicker's built there.

And to the north of them, also vacating Wicker Field and having now moved above Snake Creek into District 11 were "Calvin" and "Catherine" (or Joseph and Barbra) with their family. Why they chose to give their middle names to the census taker is unknown. Perhaps the federal census in 1870 was perceived as a "Yankee" thing and bitter feelings from the war still ran deep? As stated, the eastside of Hardin County, east of the Tennessee River at Savannah, had been more Union rather than Confederate in the fray.

Also in District 11 were Jasper and family and Mary Elizabeth Strawn and family. Roderick's widow, Catherine is also there, raising two, plus her youngest, born early-to-mid-1862 and named after his father who likely never saw him, Roderick Gaines Wicker. Catherine's oldest, Mary Lucrecia, is now married to John Strawn, living nearby. John will be done in by a discharge from his own fallen shotgun in 1871. That will set up wife, Mary, coming to Texas in 1874 and marrying this author's great grandfather in 1876.

All of the above family members are noted here as they would have undoubtedly visited, not only Elzina, but especially family matriarch, Widow Flora, at times during this era and before she died by 1880. In doing so, it is possible for them to have gone next door and visited in their old family cabin, now occupied by the George's. They had been neighbors to the Wickers there since about 1853 and at least until the George's left for first Texas and then Arkansas in the early 1870's. Even Mary, before the marriages of she and Sarah George, born only two months apart, probably became friends upon visits.

Also, it can be safely concluded that most, if not all, of Lewis Wicker's then living family members would be aware of the George's current home history, not just grandson John W. Wicker, future cabin owner later. No doubt, even all of the grandchildren were told, and especially by "Grandma Flora," when they visited her, that she and their grandfather, and/or their mothers or fathers, built the old cabin now next door. Some of that knowledge even made it to Texas.

Over time and over telling, oral family histories can change but the root of the matter is still there. Certainly all of Flora's living children in 1862 knew of the move. They would have known where their old family cabin was originally located, that they helped build and lived in after coming from Lincoln County by 1849, and, to know who bought and moved it after the battle and when and where it was moved.

A Deed and a Family History Helps Document the Cabin...

When did the George's vacate the old cabin and when did occupant Widow Sarah Bell die? On previous trips to Savannah to the Register's Office to try and trace back and complete the land ownership title where the cabin is today, a determination had never been made as to whether or not William Manse George ever actually owned the land. Speculation was that his mother-in-law only "gave" him some land to farm and build a cabin on, after he married daughter Nancy Bell, about 1852, ten years before the battle.

The history of ownership was previously traced back from the USA, to Samuel Chambers, to John W. Wicker, to O. H. P. Cantrell but then it hit a gap. It seemed he should have gotten title from the Bell family, so research was for the names Bell/Cantrell. What was discovered recently were two deeds; one to Cantrell from a Cunningham, then a deed index reference to Cunningham from "M. E. Hargrove & others." Upon looking at the instrument, "M. E." is the former Miranda E. Bell. The deed was to W. M. Cunningham and was signed by the Bell heirs in Texas in 1871 and included Wm. George and Nancy J. George, plus others. So William Manse George did own the cabin land, with others, until October 20, 1871. The Bell heirs move to Texas is in their history.

This ties down a closer time frame the George's and perhaps Sarah Bell left the cabin, and, helps identify a window of time within which Widow Sarah Bell died. In the July 11, 1870 census she is still alive and living with the George's in the cabin. Sometime thereafter and before the October 20, 1871 deed signing by her heirs in Texas, she would have died, probably in the old cabin in Tennessee. The Bell's Shiloh history does not say.

To complete the ownership, the 1871 deed was to W. M. Cunningham of Hardin County, who one month later in November, 1871 sold it to the aforementioned, O. H. P. Cantrell. Both deeds, changing cabin ownership, were not recorded until nine years later in 1880. Five years later, Cantrell sold to Wicker who sold to Chambers who sold to the USA.

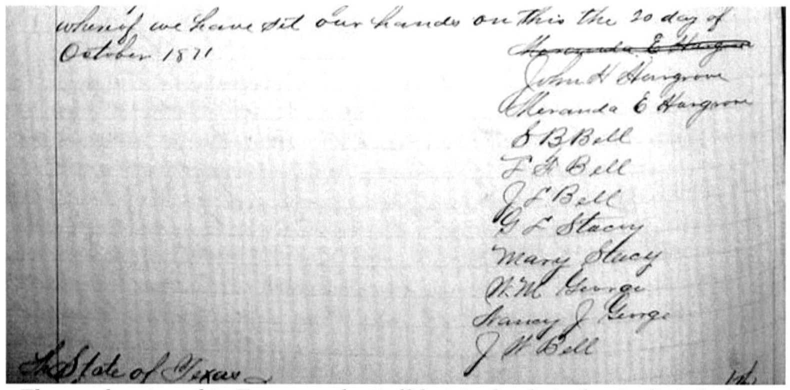
whereof we have set our hands on this the 20 day of October 1871

John H Hargrove
Meranda E Hargrove
S B Bell
J E Bell
G L Stacy
Mary Stacy
W M George
Nancy J George
J W Bell

The State of Texas

Those who signed in Texas on the Bell heir's deed. Author's digital photo.

After the July, 11, 1870 census in Hardin County, Tennessee and before the October 20, 1871 deed transaction in Texas, the George's left the cabin for Texas with the Hargroves, as it appears it was a Bell/Hargrove migration. After the signing, some went to Arkansas.

Cabin Courtin' & Connectin' – Cradles & Coffins

By now in time, at least three Wicker boys had become married when they lived in the old cabin. Then Sarah George would be courted and marry while residing in it after the war. Before that, her younger brother, James William, will be born in it by 1864. Two elderly former cabin occupants will have died by 1862 and 1871, Lewis Wicker and Widow Sarah Bell, respectively, she probably while still in the old cabin. Therefore it will have experienced in its lifetime as a home; courting and the connection of household members through marriage, then bear cradles for 'chillun' and to bier coffins for corpses.

On the frontier, there was scant opportunity for wooing and wedding. A courtship of a few weeks was considered enough time to warrant a proposal of marriage. Much of the courting took place within the confines of the one-room cabin. If parents accepted their daughter's beau, their early exit was the stamp of approval. If they disapproved of the young man's intentions, or if the daughter didn't welcome him, the parents would "sit him out" until the wee hours.[77]

Weddings in the 18th- and 19th-century South were typically brief and plain. They were held in the home rather than in a church...Most southern marriages... occurred in the morning or at noon to allow family and community to gather at the bride's house after the wedding for a meal and often dancing, music, and games. [78]

Then a "game" of the animal type is evidenced for that meal:

"On the frontier this feast had been mainly [wild] game, and the quantity depended upon the luck of the chase, but by the time farms and plantations were well established, all

[77] Beverly Downing , "I Do!," *Family Chronicle, The Magazine for Families Researching Their Roots*, http://www.familychronicle.com/MarriageCustoms.html.

[78] Carolyn Lipson-Walker, "Weddings" in _*Encyclopedia of Southern Culture*_, eds. Charles Reagan Wilson and William Ferris (Chapel Hill: University of North Carolina Press, 1989), 493. Vicki Betts, Reference Librarian, University of Texas-Tyler, e-mail message to author, September 29, 2007.

sorts of meats and vegetables in season went on the table."[79]

...the shivaree, the infare, and a pounding–18th- and 19th-century southern pre- and postnuptial traditions–were common marriage rituals extant throughout pre-industrial, rural America...The "pounding" was a gathering where furniture and food were brought to the new home by neighbors and family. The whole community was generally invited to the "infare" or "infaire"–a dinner at the bridegroom's parents' house held the day after the wedding or occasionally immediately following the wedding.

Particularly in the Upper South, newlyweds came to expect, even anticipate, a "shivaree" (derived from the Old World custom and word charivari). Friends of the bridal couple would surround their home, awakening them with rough music, shouting, and pestering until the couple invited them inside for refreshments...

In Kentucky and Tennessee it was traditional to kidnap the bride and groom on their wedding night until the abducted offered food, drink, or even money to their abductors. [80]

With these marriages came pregnancies and births:

The 18th and 19th centuries saw the amalgamation of Native American, Afro-American, and Euro-American folk remedies and beliefs in the South...Before the advent of modern hospitals, medical doctors, and adequate transportation, trained and untrained white and black midwives, granny women, or female neighbors assisted during home births. Prenatal care was almost nonexistent. Even when doctors and hospitals were available, many women in the rural South preferred to give birth at home with the help of

[79] Joe Gray Taylor, *Eating, Drinking, and Visiting in the South: An Informal History*, (Baton Rouge: Louisiana State University Press, 1982), 48. Betts, e-mail.
[80] Carolyn Lipson-Walker, "Weddings," 493.

midwives.[81]

Vicki Betts, Reference Librarian at the University of Texas-Tyler, who has Eastern Hardin County ties says, "I think…plain farming women, like those near Pittsburg Landing…would depend on each other to get through childbirth."[82]

Along with births bringing life…life also brings death. Since Lewis Wicker was deceased after 1860 and by the battle in 1862, and his family best believes he's interred in the Ledbetter Cemetery above Snake Creek, his body would have been taken from the future Wicker Field, past his old cabin on the way to be buried. In those days' neighbors along the way would have known and recognized the entourage, some perhaps even joining it, or if outside their cabins, paid their respects in passing. Before that, once Lewis had died, word would have been taken back above Snake Creek to the three family members living there. Then, some specifics about their response to death can be seen from the following:

…Immediately, family members and neighbors would stop what they were doing and gather at the house of the deceased and begin preparations for burial. Friends carrying food appeared almost immediately. As Will D. Campbell noted, "somehow in rural, Southern culture, food is always the first thought of neighbors when there is trouble."[83]

---

[81] Carolyn Lipson-Walker, "Childbirth" in _*Encyclopedia of Southern Culture*_, eds., Charles Reagan Wilson and William Ferris (Chapel Hill: University of North Carolina Press, 1989), 493. Betts, e-mail.

[82] Vicki Betts, Reference Librarian, University of Texas-Tyler (ancestors from east Hardin Co., TN), e-mail message to author.

[83] Donna W. Stansberry, "Burial Practices in Southern Appalachia," (Master of Arts in Liberal Studies thesis, Department of Cross Disciplinary Studies, East Tennessee State University, December 2004), 17, http://etd-submit.etsu.edu/etd/theses/available/etd-1112104-101034. Betts, e-mail.

The first task was to lay the body out. This consisted of washing the body and dressing it in the nicest clothes available. Because there was no way to preserve the body, everything had to be done as soon as possible and the body had to be dressed before rigor mortis set in. Close family members washed the body, dressed it, and laid it out. Most likely, women tended to women and men tended to men...

Part of the preparation involved putting silver coins on the eyes of the deceased to keep them closed. This custom resulted from the belief that when a person enters Heaven, he or she should do so with his or her eyes closed...asking for forgiveness of his or her sins. Silver was used because pennies had a tendency to turn the skin green. Rags soaked in soda water, aspirin, or camphor were kept on the face of the deceased until the "viewing" in an effort to keep the skin from losing it's color. The service usually took place the next day with the burial immediately following.

When someone died, the community not only came together to lay out the body but dug the grave and built the casket, usually free of charge. Men considered this part of their community duty and did it to show respect for the deceased.[84]

Obviously, neighbors like Manse George, the Bell boys, Hargroves, etc., may have become involved, in addition to any Wicker sons or sons-in-law available before the war. The same can be said after 1870 for the family and neighbors to Sarah Bell, if she indeed died there in the old cabin. The Wicker, Jones and Hargrove families next door would have helped. How did these families mourn? Some idea can be taken from the following:

By the 1830's Americans shifted their interests to the spiritual realm, and the focus on eternal life. Mourning

[84] Ibid, 17-18.

symbols such as angels, doves, and hands pointing heavenward reflected the softened views of death. Mourning expressions of grief reflected one's piety and gentility, shifting the focus to the mourner, and not the dead. Mourning was very visual, and lasted long after the burial of the dead loved one. In antebellum America, the decorating of the home in crape, the outfitting of the family in mourning clothing, family behavior, and remembrances created to memorialize the deceased were very important.[85]

And so the cabin family experiences continue…

A cabin has caught a chap come-a-courtin'
A connected couple a ceremony citin'
A child a clammerin' in a cradle a creakin'
A cryin' eye o'er a corpse in a coffin.
– Duane Helweg

[85] Karen Rae Mehaffey, "Mourning the Dead."

Chapter 8:
1880... The "Widows" Are Gone And Who Is In the Cabin?

As indicated, "Widow Sarah Bell" is dead by 1871 and Manse George and family have vacated the old cabin, left Tennessee for Texas and then are in the 1880 census in Sevier County, Arkansas. With them are daughter Sarah and husband Robert Hargrove.

Former cabin occupant Sarah (George) Hargrove, husband Robert, in front of the George home in Arkansas. Courtesy of "Lockesburg, The First One Hundred 1878-1978."

"Mr. and Mrs. Mansfield George came to Lockesburg from Tennessee just after the Civil War. They bought the place just across Town Creek that everyone today knows as 'George Hill,' being named after this family."[86]

However, we know the George's came to Texas first, then Arkansas, as already reported. Former cabin occupant Nancy (Bell) George died in 1916 and is buried in Idabel, McCurtain County, Oklahoma. It is not known when the old cabin mover, her husband William Manse George, died. But by the 1910 census, Nancy is shown as a widow living with son James William George in Idabel.

Apparently, Wicker family matriarch, Flora, has also died after 1870, as she is not found in the 1880 census. Does she lie in Ledbetter Cemetery north of Shiloh, beside her life's traveler and love, the cabin builder, Lewis? There are no markers that say so.

Alvis' oldest son, future cabin owner John W. Wicker, is censused with wife Martha in 1880 in Hardin County, possibly already in the cabin or on its land as a tenant. Elzina, with husband D. B. Greeny (?), is still living on Wicker Field in 1880, a neighbor to the old cabin. As neighbors, John's children and Elzina's youngest no doubt played together in or near the old cabin. Both John and his aunt are just a few dwelling units away from O. H. P. Cantrell, who sells the land where the cabin is to John W. Wicker in 1885.

Mr. Cantrell may have been living in the cabin, although, by the early 1900's he sells over 160 acres to the USA in two separate transactions and presumably the last of those contained his home. A park ownership map from the 1890's shows his ownership, and several other Cantrell's, just south, east and west of the cabin property. It is possible no one lived in the cabin after the George's, thus its state of disrepair in mid-1890. A "stick-and-dirt" chimney's lifespan of about

[86] The Looking Glass, ed./comp., Hatfield, AR, *Lockesburg The First One Hundred 1878-1978*, (Delight, AR: Alexander Printing, 1978), 67.

twenty years would bear this out.[87]

Sometime between the 1880 census and the one in 1900 (the 1890 one was mostly destroyed by fire in Washington, D. C.), Elzina and Dennis and family vacated Wicker Field next to the old cabin, owned during some of that time by John W. Wicker. Whoever was in the old cabin around 1880, if anybody, another event occurred close by that was still somewhat commonplace throughout the battlefield. "Jesse Curtis, a local farmer, found the remains of three Union soldiers near the Peach Orchard."[88]

Chicago Historical Society photo from the Larry J. Daniel book, "Shiloh."

Photo is the Sarah Bell field with the Peach Orchard beyond the rail fence to the rear. It was taken possibly in the 1880's, apparently from a tree looking over a cabin top. Although Widow Sarah Bell's was not rebuilt after the battle, as she was living by 1870 with the George's in the now moved

[87] Durbin, "Stick-and-Dirt Chimney."

[88] Timothy B. Smith, *This Great Battlefield of Shiloh*, statement in Series 4, Box 1, Folder 2, SNMP.

old ‘Wicker cabin,’ her son Samuel and family are living in one built there, by that census. It is probably his old cabin, as he moved to Texas shortly after the 1870 census. This books subject cabin is in the far background but could be out of this photo, probably to the left. However, if taken in the 1880’s, it is an older photo than one taken later of that neighboring ‘War Cabin‘ in 1895.

Author’s photo of the Peach Orchard in 2007 with replanted trees. They only live so long and have been replaced several times over the years since the battle-days trees. Known in the park today as the ‘Manse George cabin,’ it is to the left, just beyond the orchard, where it can be accessed from a parking area. General Johnston’s monument is to the right, rear.

<u>Cabin Life in the “Lost Census Era”…between 1880-1900.</u>

What was life like for cabin occupants in the “census-lost” era between 1880 and 1900? Following is an account from *Strawn*

Genealogy, compiled by Emmet Dee Strawn and published in 1970. Emmet was born in Western Hardin County in 1882, north of Snake Creek and grew up there. However, a mere watercourse that divided his 11th Civil District from the 15th Civil District, where the old cabin stood in 1880, would not see differences in lifestyles. Here are his personal memoirs (with this author's bracket inserts) from March of 1969, when he lived in Fresno, California, a far cry from his backwoods boy days west of the Tennessee River:

I appreciate very much the few letters that some of our relatives left behind that we may know something about them and the way they lived. This reminds me to make a few remarks, too. To say that I am now 86 years old, doesn't mean very much, but to compare it with other things gives a better understanding. The telephone and myself are about the same age.

The quickest way to get a doctor was by horseback. There were no hospitals within our range. Memphis and Nashville were about 100 miles away, too far to take a sick person in a wagon on a four days' journey over a bumpy road. We got our mail about once a week, when father went to town for groceries and that was usually sugar and coffee. We bought flour by the barrel (196 lbs.). We had meal ground once a week at an overshot grist mill [water ran over the top of the water wheel]. My great grandfather, I believe, built this mill [William Strawn, a "miller" in 1850], he also built the first cotton gin in our part of the County.

Father [Francis Loyd Strawn] had his own blacksmith shop. He shod his own horses, sharpened the plows, and etc. Mother [Nancy "Nannie" Strawn] had the cards for making bata [sic - batten] for quilts and rolls from cotton and wool for making yarn. I remember my homespun clothes, the old spinning wheel and loom that was soon pushed aside. In the first 10 years of my life many changes were taking place.

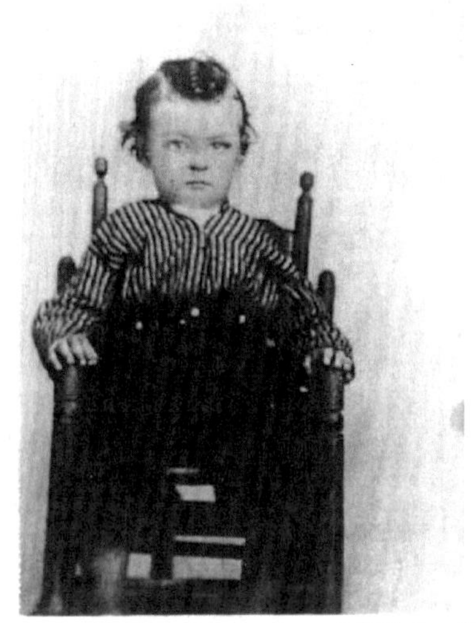

Example of "homespun clothes," per circa 1873 family photo of Loyd Gaines Strawn

The home was a place of industries. Among our relatives most everything was made. They had a tan yard–harness and shoes were made.

Man tanning leather in a loft[89]

[89] "Department of Conservation Photograph Collection, 1937-1976," *Tennessee Virtual Archive (TeVA).*

Molasses were [sic] made and I have never seen [tasted] any better not even today on the market. Everyone had a smoke-house, where the meat was cured. The good old hickory smoked hams [are] almost a thing of the past, but they still have it back at home as a luxury.

150 year-old smoke house in Sumner Co., Tennessee (underneath protective roof)[90]

Many things then the towns didn't have. You might be surprised if I said there wasn't [sic] any grocery stores. There wasn't [sic] but they had General Merchandise Stores with a few groceries that you could just about put in a wheel-barrow. A babies dress then was about two yards long.

There was much to do then in a home. My parents, besides raising us 8 children, raised two more ['Dupree' nephews per the 1880 census], whose mother died. They were treated just like we were and they never knew the difference as for treatment. One went to college and the other remained on

[90] Retreat and Vacation Homes in Sumner County, Tennessee, "Stay Down on the Farm," http://www.staydownonthefarm.com/around.php.

the farm. Mother at first had a colored maid, but later changed to a white woman, who lived with us. Her name was Mary.

I guess that I am the only person living who remembers the hand stick. They [were] in a set of 6 or 8 and were used in carrying logs in clearing land for cultivation. They were made of white hickory or oak, the strongest of wood. They were larger in the middle and tapered off at each end, just right for a hand hold. Eight men could carry a good sized log to pile to burn. This was called "log rolling." Neighbors came in and it didn't cost anything – you just returned the favor. I recall seeing a few log houses built. It was interesting to see how skilled they were in notching them in. And you have missed something if you have never seen a woman using the cards and the spinning wheel. It was a fine art and the old wheel would buzz – you could hear it a few hundred yards away. The old oaken bucket was in the well, but a brass bound cedar bucket was in the house.

In my childhood days in school, I remember a piece of poetry. I will give a part of it:

Baby bye here's a fly.
We will watch him, you and I.
How he crawls up the wall,
Yet he never falls.
I do believe with six such legs
That you and I could walk on eggs.

This was in the old McGuffy [sic] First Reader. To the child this was a mystery and I think it was to the teacher also, but now the secret of the fly has been revealed.

The following is another poem familiar to many of us. It was from the McGuffy [sic] Second Reader.

Twinkle, twinkle little star.

How I wonder what you are,
Up above the world so high,
Like a diamond in the sky.

Now we don't wonder so much for we are going up and looking them over.

Now I wonder how a mother with eight or ten children could get up at four or five o'clock in the morning and go through the day and be relaxed at night.

There were no tranquillizers then. I never saw an aspirin tablet until after I left home. My parents had a way of handling us children. It must have been love and patience. Here is one example of how mother took care of me. It was a rainy evening and I was in the kitchen hanging after her while she was trying to prepare dinner. She told me to go in the front room, lay on the floor and look under the door and watch the raindrops patter on the door steps. I did and the next thing I remember I woke up in bed the next morning. My parents lived in harmony. I never saw either one ever whip any of us children or ever heard a cross word between them.

I recall very vividly one Sunday morning my parents came out in the breezeway of our old home and sang from a hymn book (Christian Harmony), "Sweet Hour of Prayer." I thought that it was the best music that I had ever heard. We had no recordings then, only it was recorded in my heart, but I can't sing like they could. They both were good singers and we children could sing well. As we grew up, we would sing every week, usually on Saturday night with my oldest sister at the piano. We would sing hymns, folk songs, country and western music:

"Old Wooden Rocker," "Home on the Range", etc.

We not only had good parents, we had good neighbors. Dear old Mandy Layton [close by per 1880 census]. When I was a child, I had the croup and was choking to death. Mother couldn't stand it and handed me over to Mrs. Layton who was there to help. She threw me all the way to the ceiling and I caught my breath. Another neighbor was Uncle Dave Pickens, who prayed for me that I might know Christ and I did by delayed action. He was known by all as Uncle Dave. I never knew one thing wrong about him.

A good life is determined by the quality of it's memories. Pity the man whose memories haunt with terror and regret instead of giving abiding joy. If we have lived reasonably well the recollection of the past should not hurt us much but give us pleasure. One of the nicer things about memories is that sharing them does not diminish them either in number or vividness. It enhances and restores them.

I lived through the "Gay Nineties" and the "Roaring Twenties."

Every ten years of my life I could see rapid changes. The first ten years sawmills came in and sawed the logs that had been burned in the past. People began to build framed houses. Everyone had fireplaces, no heating stoves. Our old house had two fireplaces. Father built a new home with four fireplaces.

The insurance man said that it was the finest house between Adamsville and Hamburg, a distance of twelve miles. It is a good home today, but some changes have been made. Most of the timber came from our own land, nice clear oak for the foundation, red gum for the framework and poplar for siding. The shingles were cypress. Not far away is the cemetery. The land was donated by a member of our family. Some of the first settlers are buried there. More land has been donated by a neighbor and no charge has ever been made for a lot.

We speak of the good old days and they were good, but there were many inconveniences and hardships. Then, we didn't have a bath tub, but we boys had [the] Tennessee River and it was [all] about private – no homes along the shore, but we had land along the river. We never had heard of a bathing suit then and we didn't need one. Sometimes a steamboat would go by and the pilot would wave at us and the waves from the boat would make us bob up and down.

The home place is modern now – running hot and cold water. I still visit there every year or two. I may make my last trip this year. Things have changed rapidly since my birth and are still changing. It has changed from long hours of hard work to a push button system. Should I ask myself the question of which I would choose, I would choose today. Leave out the hard work and live longer. Sanitation and medical science has added much to our life span. As a child, life expectancy was about forty-five years. Now it is seventy, and I am enjoying these extra years. When I was a child, neighbors would help when needed. Now the government takes over. We are living in the Atomic Age, the most prosperous time in history.

The farmers all had kerosene lanterns. They took them to the barn each morning to feed the stock, milk the cows and do other chores. On Sunday there was no work. They worked six days of twelve or fourteen hours with time out to go to town to bring home the coffee. It was green and had to be parched at home, usually in a dutch [sic] oven on the fireplace. The dutch [sic] oven then stood up on three legs about three inches long. The lid had a rim around the edge curled up about an inch, and an eye handle in the center so that you could take a fire hook and lift it off. You could shovel coals of fire underneath or on the lid. It was fine for baking.

...I would like to say something about the old ash-hopper that disappeared from our back yard [meaning no longer used] about the time that I was grown. Now the word has disappeared from our language. It was built oblong, about three by five feet. Four forked posts were put in the ground and poles were laid in the forks. They were called ash-hoppers forks. You would take a froe [wedge] and rive (split) some four

foot boards to lay against the poles with the lower ends resting in a wooden trough dug from a log with no joints but one end open. Thus the hopper was formed. You would put the winter's ashes from the fireplaces and fill the hopper. In the spring you would pour water on the ashes and lye would run down the trough into an iron kettle partly buried in the ground. You would then fill a twenty gallon kettle with the lye and start boiling. You would take fat meat scraps gathered from the smoke house and add to the lye which would eat the scraps up and which would weaken the lye. Mother would test it occasionally and if it were too strong, she would add more fat. The means of testing were taking a chicken feather, dipping it in the lye and pulling it between thumb and finger. If it stripped clean, leaving only the stem or quill, it was done.

Ash Hopper, George Washington Carver National Monument, National Park Service, Diamond, Missouri. Online photo.

Then it was poured into a sixty gallon barrel in the smoke house. This was continued until the barrel was about full. This was a year's supply and no better soap could be had. It was in a jell form and used for everything where soap was needed. I doubt very much if there is any better today.

However, some today is perfumed. I recall when a lad we needed to replace the forks. I yoked up two good sized calves, hitched them to a sled and went to the woods and cut four more ash-hopper forks. It may be news to you, but you never used a harness on an ox or oxen. You used the yoke only and a whip if they didn't obey.

There were no railroads there. I never saw a train until I was almost grown. I could hear the train whistle eighteen miles away. Why should we leave our community for we had everything there. We received our freight by boat. I was a country boy...

E. D. Strawn[91]

Overshot Mill on Snake Creek as shown in Tim Smith's book, "The Untold Story of Shiloh." Picture from SNMP archives.

Author's note: One interesting side story that harkens back to April 6, 1862, when General Lew Wallace was trying to get to Shiloh from the north and west, involves an "overshot

[91] Emmet Dee Strawn, compiler, *Strawn Genealogy*, self-published, 1970.

mill," as Mr. Strawn referred to it in his above memoirs. Following is the story from Larry Daniel's *Shiloh, the Battle That Changed the Civil War*:

Wallace did not know precisely how to get to the River Road from his present location, short of returning to the crossroads just outside Stoney Lonesome. He dispatched his orderlies to bring in a local guide, forcibly if necessary…Wallace's orderlies eventually found a farmer by the name of Dick Pickens who lived by Overshot Mill.[92]

Based on research, this was apparently the overshot mill built by William Strawn by at least 1850. The Pickens is Richard, about age 20, son of Hezekiah Pickens mentioned earlier in this work. This has been confirmed by a Pickens descendant.

[92] Larry J. Daniel, *Shiloh: The Battle that Changed the Civil War* (New York: Touchstone/Simon & Shuster, 1997), 260.

Chapter 9: Park History And The 1890s...

As stated, Alvis' son, John W. Wicker, buys the cabin land next to Wicker Field in 1885, maybe even when the Green's are still living on that field since it is only known they left by the end of the century as the park development began to occur. Here's that history:

Between 1890 and 1899 the Congress of the United States went well beyond the concept of monuments and authorized the establishment of four major battlefields of the Civil War as national military parks. In so doing, it laid one of several foundation stones for the national historic preservation policy and program we have today. These four battlefields were Chickamauga and Chattanooga authorized in 1890, Shiloh in 1894, Gettysburg in 1895, and Vicksburg in 1899.[93]

Since its creation in 1916, the National Park Service has been charged with promoting and regulating the use of areas within the National Park System...Originally established under the War Department in 1894, Shiloh National Military Park was transferred to the administration of the NPS in 1933...For two thirds of its length, Shiloh Battlefield's 1894

[93] Ronald F. Lee, *The Origin and Evolution of the National Military Park Idea*, 1973, National Park Service, http://www.nps.gov/history/history/online_books/history_military. Chapter III, 1.

authorized boundary line follows the watercourses around "Shiloh Hill," a rolling plateau rising above the surrounding Tennessee River bottomlands. A strong defensive position, Shiloh Hill became the campsite for General Grant's forces in March 1862, and thus the focus of the Confederate attack on April 6th & 7th. The park's authorized boundary encloses about 6000 acres, of which two-thirds are currently in Federal ownership.[94]

As the old cabin lies in ruin and awaiting its fate, the following transcriptions from the *Savannah Courier* show this about the battlefield establishment that will change the cabins history. References to names like, "Cherry, Nisbet and City of Paducah" are boats:

Feb 22, 1894 - Shiloh Battlefield: The following taken from the National Tribune, Washington, D. C...

*} **Col. E. T. Lee**, Secretary of the Shiloh Battlefield Association, of Monticello, Ill., is in the city. He is here to make a report to the house committee, composed of **Col. D. B. Henderson** of Iowa; **Gen. Joseph Wheeler** of Alabama,and **John C. Black** of Illinois; also the Senate Committee, composed of **Senators Isham G. Harris**, of Tennessee; **John Sherman** of Ohio; **W. P. Vials** of Wisconsin. The report covers the proceedings of the Association from its organization, and includes a report of the committee that visited the battlefield and secured options on the land which the association desires the Government purchase for a grand memorial Park, and the graves of the soldiers there be preserved. The association is meeting with great encouragement in their efforts. There is a universal sentiment all over the country that this old historic*

---

[94] SNMP, *Park Administration and History*, http://www.nps.gov/archive/shil/admlpp.htm.

battlefield, where was fought the first great open field battle in the West, should be preserved.

The old Army of the Tennessee, have none of the battlefields preserved, and they claim Shiloh.

***Secretary Lee** has received thousands of letters from the old survivors from all parts of the country urging that this battlefield be preserved, and he has the names and post office address of 1,000 of the survivors of that battle. Many of these will attend the reunion on the battlefield next April 6 and 7, and assist the association in marking the positions held by their commands during the battle of the 6th and 7th, 1862.*

It is requested that each command prepare a marker of some kind to place at these positions. It has been suggested that for the present a one-inch board 10 by 18 be painted white, with the letters and number in black, to nail to the trees until more permanent markers can be placed there by the Government, the States, or the various associations that took part in the battle. All are invited to the reunion on next April 6 and 7 to assist in this work.

*Mar 22, 1894 - Shiloh Battlefield: A letter from **E. T. Lee**, of Monticello, Ill., who is secretary of the Shiloh Battlefield Association, informs us that all arrangements are about complete for the grand reunion at the Shiloh Battlefield on April 6th and 7th. The Association committee that visited Washington in December was presented to the Congressional Committee and believes that a bill will soon be introduced for an appropriation to purchase the ground on which this famous battle was fought, with good prospects for its early passage.*

No fancy prices will be paid for the land on which the battle was fought, but the committee will treat all alike. Parties who own these lands that have not yet given the committee options should do so during the reunion. The committee headquarters will be on the W. F. Nisbet.

The railroads and steamboats have all made liberal reductions in rates, and the steamboats will lay at the landing and furnish meals and lodgings as far as possible. Visitors who cannot be accommodated by the steamboats will be carried by the steamers to Savannah, where the hotels will provide lodgings and meals.

All the good people of Hardin County and Savannah are invited to be present.

This invite certainly drew locals to the old cabin area. Some, including those living within the future park, would have known its history and shared with out-of-state guests.

Apr 12, 1894 - A Pleasant Reunion: The Blue and Gray Meet on Equal Footing. On April 6th and 7th, 1862, Hardin county was drenched with the blood of brothers who had met at Shiloh in deadly combat. On the 6th the two armies met about two miles south of Pittsburg Landing, the Confederates completely surprising the Union army which was forced to retreat as they fought till late at night when both sides rested on their arms.

The morning of the 7th found the Union forces greatly re-enforced and on that day it was the Confederates who retreated as they fought over the ground won the day before. All know how the battle ended in a victory for the Union soldiers.

} An organization was recently formed, known as the Shiloh Battlefield Association, and is composed of ex-soldiers of both armies which has in view the purchase of all the lands on which the battle was fought and the conversion of the same into a memorial park. The association is only in its infancy but we have great confidence in its ultimate success. The reunion on the 6th and 7th was inaugurated by this association, and of its success all who attended will testify.

The distinguished characters present at the reunion were:

Gen. Lew Wallace, *author of Ben Hur and other*

famous writings, and on whose shoulder was put the blame of the defeat of the Federals on the first day.

It was claimed that he was all day marching five miles, but a careful survey of his line of march shows that travel 18 and 1/4 miles with an army of 7,000 men. ***Gen. John A. McClernand****, who is president of the association;* ***Gen. Wm. T. Shaw****, who gained fame in the "Hornets Nest" fight;* ***Gen. Sam McGinnis****, and* ***Col. E. T. Lee****, secretary of the association, all of the Union army.* ***Gen. J. R. Chalmers****, who led the Confederate right and so completely routed the left wing of the Union army was the only Confederate general present.*

Able and conciliatory, speeches were made by ***McClernand, Chalmers, Lee, Wallace*** *and others. The number of visitors of the grounds was probably between 2,500 and 3,000, each day. The number registering in the cemetery office for the two days was 455.*

Although apparently the old cabin lay in ruin (based on future park pictures from 1895), the above men may well have seen it as they visited such as the Peach Orchard and walked the Sunken Road. Discussion and knowledge of its history may have ensued.

Apr 26, 1894 - A charter of the Shiloh Battlefield Association has been forwarded to the Secretary of State by ***James Williams****, the assistant Secretary of the South.*

*June 14, 1894 - ...****Col. E. T. Lee****, Secretary of the Shiloh Battlefield Association, got off the Nisbet last week and remained over here and at Pittsburg Landing till the City of Savannah went down. He practically completed the work of taking options on all the lands included in the field, so that the work can proceed to completion as soon as appropriation is made by Congress, which is now...under way.*

Dec 13, 1894 - The Shiloh Battlefield Association: The Shiloh(Part of this is missing) for the purchase of the *battlefield and the improvement of the same parcel passed the House of Representatives on Dec 4, without a dissenting vote, and will certainly pass the Senate in a short time and become a law. The bill gives the Commission $75,000 for the commencement of the work, which is all that will be needed until the next congress meets. This is one of the greatest achievements that has been carried through and means much for Hardin county and the State of Tennessee. I have given it my undivided time and have put in the best work of my life on this matter and have the right to feel justly proud of the results. As soon as the Commission is appointed and organized the work of securing the lands and settling for the same will begin. The coming reunion on April 6 to 12, 1895, will be an immense gathering and will be attended by many from all parts of the Union. The various positions will be marked and all disputed points settled. Let all prepare for this gathering of the Blue and Gray, on the border of the historic Tennessee.* ***E. T. Lee****, Secty, Monticello, Ill., Shiloh B. Ass. Dec 7, 1894.*

Feb 28, 1895 - ***Capt. J. W. Irwin****, the Government agent to purchase the land for the Shiloh Memorial Park, passed up on the Cherry Tuesday, to begin the work to at once.*

Mar 7, 1895 - ***Maj. Davis****, of the war records office, will be down this week to assist* ***Capt. Irwin*** *in establishing the boundary of the National Park.*

} County Surveyor ***Harbert*** *and crew, with* ***Capt. Irwin****, Government Purchasing Agent, commenced the survey of the National Park at Pittsburg Landing on Tuesday. They will first locate the boundary, or outside lines of the Park, then a separate survey of each tract or parcel on the inside of the park will be made. Owing to the fact a large portion of the battlefield is very hilly and rough, it will ...require several weeks to complete the entire survey.*

} ***Robert Hardin*** *came in on the Paducah Tuesday from Nashville, to assist in the survey of the National Park at*

Pittsburg Landing.[95]

Thus the stage is set for the War Department Battlefield Commission to have determined the validity of the old cabin's history and its viability for preservation. Anyone visiting the old cabin at any of the *Savannah Courier* articles dates or times would have found it belonging to John W. Wicker, either residing in another cabin on the premises with his family, or, perhaps next door on Wicker Field. Of course, other people were living about, on the future park lands but at some point, cabin land owner John W. Wicker, and even other of his neighbors, would have conveyed the cabin's history to the men of the Commission, or any others who came to visit and make inquiry of it.

For whomever of those men, albeit one or many, it is commended at this time their foresight in realizing then that the battleground was more than just the armies that gathered there to do battle. Private citizens homes and lands and lives became part of its history on that momentous occasion of April 6 and 7, 1862.

During this same era, the *Courier* reported on the controversial documentation afield, not far from the old cabin, which took place regarding the spot where General Johnston died:

Apr 9, 1896 - ***Senator Isham G. Harris*** *was at Shiloh last week, and succeeded in marking the spot where* ***Gen. Albert S. Johnston*** *fell. The venerable Senator was* ***Johnston's*** *chief of staff officer and assisted that gallant Confederate chieftain from his horse when he received the mortal wound.*

[95] Edward R. Harrell, transcriber, *Savannah Courier,* newspaper published in Hardin County, Savannah, Tennessee, transcriptions, 1885-1901, donated to the project, http://www.tngenweb.org/hardin, sub-selection on rootsweb at ancestry.com, years utilized, 1894 -1899.

*The place as recognized by **Senator Harris** is altogether different from that supposed to be the scene of **Johnston's** dying moments.*

Then two years later:

*Apr 8, 1898 - } **John P. Broom** of Hickman county, was here Wednesday on his way to Shiloh to again view that famous battlefield which bears so much of interest to him. He was **Gen. Albert Sidney Johnston's** orderly, being only 18 years old at the time, and was by his side on the day Johnston was killed, and probably knows more of the circumstances of the death of that famous southern general than any man living. He does not agree with the late **Senator Harris** as to the locality of the death, and thinks he can produce unquestioned authority as to the correctness of his position. He has a number of relatives in this and McNairy County, and will be in this section several days.*

Timothy B. Smith, in his book, *The Untold Story of Shiloh*, helps to clarify at least the Johnston death location issue over tree, versus ravine, which will be detailed later. General Johnston actually died in a ravine.[96]

Since the 1890 census was lost to fire, perhaps the following numbers were taken from it beforehand, where one can take a "bird's eye" view of the park and the old cabin in 1898 from this transcribed excerpt from the *Courier*:

Feb 11, 1898 - Shiloh Park: Perhaps most of the readers of the Courier have visited this historic place, but for the benefit of those who have not, we will say that it is situated in the 15th Civil District of Hardin County, Tenn., nine miles from Savannah, twenty-two miles from Corinth, Miss., and

[96] Timothy B. Smith, *The Untold Story of Shiloh: The Battle and the Battlefield* (Knoxville: The University of Tennessee Press, 2006), 35.

twenty miles from Selmer.

About thirty six years ago grim visaged war held high carnival here, but today the white winged Angel of Peace broods over us and finds us with the following: Two stores, two post offices, three telephone offices, two graded schools, three churches, two gins, two mills, one saw mill, two black smith shops, one doctor, 4 preachers, twelve teachers, two civil engineers, two magistrates, one constable, four photographers, four widows, two widowers, 12 young ladies, 12 young men and children galore, two hundred cannon, ten thousand cannon balls, and a population about ten thousand but the sad part of the population is that most of the inhabitants sleep the sleep that knows no waking. Our visitors are legion - over ten thousand annually.

The cabin at this time was perhaps still undergoing its first preservation by the War Department as it had been purchased by them, just over two months before, on the previous December 1, 1897. The visitor numbers mentioned, which may have started occurring as early as 1894, could have at least visually seen the old cabin in its then historical state, including when preservation began to occur, and, through even tenancy at some point. All during this time, even with people still living around the park and specifically the cabin area, those visitors would have been stopping at the now infamous Peach Orchard and Bloody Pond nearby, plus some undoubtedly walking the also now famous Sunken Road to view the 'Hornet's Nest' as it were at that time.

In stopping at and visiting all mentioned, no doubt the old cabin was seen, even visited, in whatever state it was in at the time and even with tenants there. In fact, the number of visitor's stopping by the old cabin, and potential interference with the daily lives of those living there, may have caused the War Department (due to complaining disturbed tenants) to eventually give up the further renting of it out to anyone.

Purchase and Park Preservation Begins.

The USA (initially War Department) began buying land in 1896, after park establishment. At the time of park inception, 1894, John W. Wicker still owned the cabin and land thereon. An early USA park map of ownership showed what John had, as "J. W. Wicker" is printed across his portion. It is in the shape of today's state of Oklahoma. The bulk of it included about three-fourths of Bloody Pond, plus the land where the cabin now stands, and, some of the famous Peach Orchard. A narrow strip forms the panhandle that crosses Hamburg-Savannah Road and runs east.

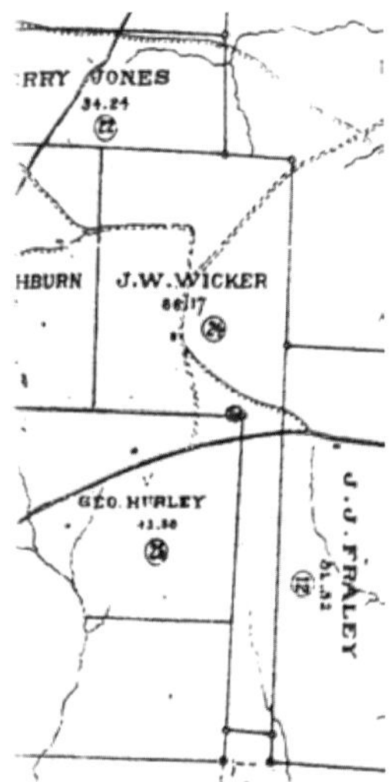

North is to the right - note 'Jones' and 'Fraley.' Courtesy of SNMP.

In a War Department photo, taken about 1895, as was marked on the photocopy which was scanned from those provided out of park files, if today's cabin, it was in horrible unlivable condition at that time. The roof had collapsed, chinking was gone as was the dirt part of the 'stick and dirt' chimney and while one can see the two doors (one through the 'chinkless' walls) there is no window adjacent to that chimney?

However, if it is the cabin, since John W. Wicker owned the property the old cabin was on at that time, he must have shared then with War Department Battlefield Commission, developing the park, the history of the cabin. This would include who built it, who bought it after the battle and moved it and when. The importance of that history had to have been noted and decided upon at some point for the War Department to bother to salvage, attempt to restore, preserve and rebuild the old cabin. Why else would they take a picture of a dwelling in such a state of ruin? Otherwise, in its shape, removal would be the order of the day, once they owned the land it was on by 1897, although not recorded until 1899.

Chimney side of the cabin in 1895. Courtesy SNMP.
(#22 on tree trunk is a 'glass plate negative number')

If the present owner when the picture was taken, John W. Wicker, grandson to Lewis Wicker, would know and recall the old cabin's history some 40 years later for a 1934 park research paper writer, he certainly knew the same in the mid-1890's when Congress established the park. At that time, the

War Department would have been deciding the importance of all that was to be within Shiloh National Military Park.

In addition, remaining members in the park area of the Bell and Jones families, either upon whose lands family members moved the cabin or helped move it, would certainly all know and remember that history and be able to share it with the War Department. This would especially be true of Perry Clark Jones, who, as reported, personally helped Manse George move the logs. He will even be indicated as being a park employee by 1899.[97]

As land began to be purchased for the park, persons living there could remain for their lifetimes if they chose. This strung out the possession process for the War Department until those living there either moved of their own volition or died. Thus the development process spanned over several decades and even after the National Park Service took over in 1933. Deed transfers took place as late as 1934. Some private parties were not gone from the park lands until as late as the 1950's, per former park ranger Tim Smith. The physical park development began where it could, especially after 1900.

Even prior to then, development was reported by the *Savannah Courier* when it indicates the arrival of some of the park's military hardware, some probably placed near the cabin:

Mar 5, 1897 - The City of Paducah [a ship] put off two hundred cannon at Pittsburg Landing Tuesday, that will be used on the Shiloh Battlefield to mark the location of the different batteries during the great battle of 1862.

Mar 12, 1897 - } Cannon For Shiloh: The City of Paducah, on her last trip had, for Shiloh Park 188 guns, weighing 267,500 pounds. There were twenty-four 30 pounders, Parrott rifles; 40 twelve pounder Howitzers and 122 six pound, bronze guns. They are to mark the places where the

[97] Smith, *This Great Battlefield of Shiloh*, 104.

different batteries stood when the battle was fought. For freight on the cargo the boat gets about $650.

Considering the potential from an undertaking of this magnitude for the day, that development would not be without personal injuries and loss of life. Even before 1900, again the *Courier* reports:

May 5, 1899 – } Resolution Of Respect: Whereas, God in his just dispensation took instantly from our midst, Mar 31, 1899, by the falling of a rock while loading a wagon with gravel on the Shiloh National Park, our friend and brother, ***Walter****, the son of* ***Pinkney and Mary Washburn****. He was born in McNairy County, Tenn. In the summer of 1880 he professed faith in Christ, and became a member of the M. E. Church, South at Shiloh...*

Perhaps the loading of gravel that killed the young man was going to be used for the graveled road and walkway that exists today at the old cabin to give better access. At that time it could have been undergoing preservation to allow the subsequent tenancy that occurred there by at least 1905, if not as early as the above 1899 date, or before.

Author's note: It should be noted that before the War Department could start buying lands, ownerships had to be established and property boundaries defined on the ground. If you recall, on deeds from the 1850's, trees were named and "marked" as those boundaries or "pointed" to them. During the battle, the intense artillery fire, plus fires that started, destroyed many of such trees. Therefore it is understandable when Ranger Tim Smith first reported to this author the difficulty the War Department had in determining who owned what and where. Even a survey done on a Tilghman property around 1870, in this author's attempt to trace a location by, relative to those deeds at the park entrance, had a wrong direction "call" by the surveyor.

2007 picture taken by the author from the graveled cabin approach.

Chapter 10: The Old Cabin Witnesses A Different Battle

Upon a first visit to Shiloh and inquiry about the Wicker's, in the year 2000, an older park ranger at the Visitor Center desk told of a feud between the Wicker's and Joneses. Apparently a Wicker boy had shot a Jones man. The government was afraid the two families might wipe each other out before they could get them paid and moved off the park lands. The incident occurred right next to the old cabin and involves one of Alvis Wicker's sons, James Wicker, and Perry Clark Jones and his son, Charles Perry Jones.

In Ranger Tim Smith's book on administrative history he chronicles the story, apparently from park records. Here's what he wrote:

There was even a murder when, on January 14, 1899, Perry Jones, a park employee, got into a family disturbance with "one of the Wicker boys." Wicker shot and killed Jones, whereupon Perry Jones's son stabbed Wicker four times. Atwell Thompson reported, "I presume that some of the Wicker relations will kill young Jones, and the two families [will be] 'wiped out' before they get through."[98]

---

[98] Ibid.

This author disagrees with some of the park's reporting, on both the sequence and what happened, per research of court records and family input. Based on who went to trial (James Wicker) and the charge (1st degree murder), the incident apparently follows more family history reporting. That states James Wicker confronted both Joneses at the elder one's home. Both Joneses stabbed Wicker and he in turn shot the older Jones.

Charles Jones never stood trial for his part, that could be found, and that, together with the fact Wicker received a 'not guilty' verdict, begs of self-defense. There was a "killing" but not a "murder," as reported, which requires malice aforethought. If you recall, the older Jones was the one who helped the George's move the cabin logs in 1862.

Union School in the late 1890's. Courtesy of Nina (Wicker) Anderson. (Rufus Wicker, standing left; note the obliterated faces of the two 'Jones')

This author has made a connection here in Texas with a cousin named Nina (Wicker) Anderson. She told some of the story as it was her uncle, James, who was involved. Also, she provided a picture of Union School in this same era, located just up the road, north, from the old cabin. James may have lived with the old cabins owner, who was his oldest brother, John, or, next door with their father, Alvis, on Wicker Field.

The Joneses were neighbors there next door, per 1890's park maps (see map shown earlier), and a Jones son was the teacher, and another a student, along with two Wicker students. Interestingly, the faces of both Joneses have been obliterated in the school picture, due to the incident.

Charlie Jones was the teacher and bad blood apparently started earlier over the romance and subsequent secret marriage in October of 1898 between him and an older Alvis Wicker daughter, Julia. It's an almost "Hatfield-McCoy" type of feud. Following is the detailed story from an interview of James son, plus input from other family members:

Charlie taught James and there was a confrontation at school. James was eating nuts and getting hulls on the floor and when teacher Jones objected and confronted him about it, fisticuffs ensued. In some later timeframe, Rufus (Nina's father), went by wagon to the Jones home to retrieve some corn from Perry Jones (who had a grist mill). He was refused the corn and was upset and went home in tears. James got the gun, returned by the mule-drawn wagon and both Joneses were there. After a confrontation about the corn, James picked up the un-ground corn, slung it over his shoulder and started back to the wagon.

He heard footsteps, turned and faced Perry Jones who was wielding a knife in one hand and a rock in the other. He threw the rock, striking James in the head. James dropped the corn and reached in his overall pocket for the gun. Son Charlie, in the meantime, had circled around, came from behind, and he, also, began stabbing him. Perry grabbed both James shoulders and tried to cut the arm holding the gun.

James put the gun against Perry and fired. The bullet lodged in a ball of wax, (thought the wax was used on twine?) in Mr. Jones pocket, he fired once again, and that killed him on this January 14, 1899. Then James fell to the ground bleeding from his knife cuts. Charlie then fled either to the Wickers to get Julia, or from within his house and they left for Texas (but returned later).

After recovering enough later to speak, James reported to his family members that after the shooting, Perry's wife came out of the house, knelt down next to his and her husband's bodies, placed her mate's head on her lap and said, "I've picked you up all these years, and now I'll pick you up for the last time."

Someone, perhaps Mrs. Jones and offspring, then put James in the wagon, untied the mules and they came home on their own, with James blood dripping from the back of the wagon. A doctor came and treated him, but told them he wouldn't live as he had lost too much blood. An elderly black former slave lady, who helped Mrs. Wicker in the home, came and said she would stay with the Wickers, as she had a name for nursing people back to health. James son said she fed him chicken soup and "rot-gut" whiskey and would have him taken outside (weather permitting) on a mattress to lie in the sunshine. Others in the family, who provided information, said she had some "weird stuff" she cooked and James ate.

It took many months to recover (delayed the trial), according to James son. He said later on, Rufus was plowing and James was bringing him a drink of water when someone (Charlie suspected) tried to shoot James. He got hit by buckshot in the shoulder (one remained against his shoulder blade), one went thru his hat, and another through an ear. James tried to run on a lame leg as best he could to cut off the perpetrator but Rufus ran and tackled his brother to keep him from getting killed. After that, James was given a permit to carry a gun. Charlie and Julia supposedly left everything there, and came to Texas. [However, if they did, they had returned before May of 1899 as indicated below. They did go to Texas, once, before permanently settling there, based on their children's birthplaces.]

In a letter of December 1902, postmarked "Hamburg, Tennessee," Noel Durbin wrote the Wickers in Texas. He was James friend and a former neighbor's son in Tennessee to the Wickers, per the 1900 census (and is also Lear Durbin's brother). In that letter he asked of James, "Did he ever get stout, and did he ever get over that lameness in his leg?" James had a bad limp the rest of his life because of the incident. Julia was not welcomed by the "Wicker boys," at Rufus funeral in Texas in 1937. They just could not forgive and forget...

Much of this story holds up from research and obtaining the circuit court minutes in Volume K & L, Feb. 1900 – Mar. 1907, from the case in the county seat of Savannah, Tennessee. It was Case No. 9, State of Tennessee vs. James Wicker on a charge of murder in the 1st degree. On October 13, 1900, in a trial by jury, James Wicker was found "Not Guilty" (or "No-billed," per James son). Also found on microfilm was a chancery court case from May of 1899 to resolve the estate of Perry Clark Jones, who died intestate (without a will) on January 14, 1899. His son C. P. Jones was the administrator and complainant against family members and others named as defendants. The deceased Jones ran a cotton gin and grist mill in partnership with a neighbor, J. R. Washburn. This holds to the above story about the corn. The gun used in the incident remains with a family descendant in Texas.

This story is included in the cabin history as it witnessed some of the incidents therein. In fact, whoever was in the now presumably restored cabin would have heard the gunshots. Maybe Alvis lived in the renovated cabin as he and John are one dwelling number apart in the June, 1900 census?

John W., either lived on the property where the old cabin still remained, or, he and his father were occupying the two cabins now vacated next door on Wicker Field. The old cabin property was bordered mostly on the west side by the Jones property and bordered mostly on the north side by Wicker Field ('Fraley' on map), thus lay on land occupied by, or in between, the two feuding families. Even though the Jones property abutted the cabins, access to the Jones property was from a road west of the Hamburg-Savannah one where the cabin property and Wicker Field had access.

Author's photo of actual gun used – .38 caliber, Smith & Wesson Safety Hammerless, 4th model, 1898 issue – A 5 shot break top with 3 1/4" barrel

Although both John's property and Wicker Field had been sold by 1900 to the USA, apparently the occupants remained as tenants. This fits the ranger's original feud description given. Alvis may have remained a tenant until he moved to Texas after James trial that October or at least by December 1902, as the letter referenced previously is dated. John may have actually remained a tenant there until through at least the 1930 census, detailed later, on the same land as the old cabin, or, next door on Wicker Field.

Although this author disapproves of the shooting incident, one must also confess to another improper family event that occurred near the old cabin. Some of the "Wicker boys" were responsible for taking bark from the tree (there were two separately identified) near where Confederate

General Albert Sidney Johnston died. The boys in turn sold the bark as a souvenir to willing buyers, probably at times right in front of or out of the old cabin. At some point, as time passed and the trees eventually were stripped (before the park fenced them), the bark sold may not have even been from those trees. Neither tree exists today, but Johnston's death place is located just south, and across the Hamburg-Savannah Road, not far from the old cabin, as stated.

However, the boys weren't the only ones taking advantage of that situation as the *Savannah Courier* reports from a Memphis newspaper, although questionable itself:

Feb 4, 1898 - A Sacred Relic: ***J. A. Parrish****, now of this city, but who was raised near the battlefield at Shiloh, has in his possession a small piece of oak which came from the stump against which* ***Isham G. Harris*** *laid the body of* ***Gen. Albert Sidney Johnston*** *after he died in his arms. Some time ago the stump was dug up by the owner of the land on which it stood, and it was cut into pieces about two inches long, and these pieces sold. At last spring's celebration there he is said to have sold $260 worth of this relic.*

- Memphis Commercial Appeal

May 13, 1898 - } Shiloh Park: The government is preparing to build a fence around the trees where ***Gen. A. S. Johnston*** *died, to protect them from intruders. The fence is to be made of barbed wire, and will be eight feet high.*[99]

Note the plural "trees" indicated in the above. As reported earlier, Johnston actually died in a ravine. One of the trees fenced was located there. The other was located on a hill nearby that Harris verified and the War Department nailed a

[99] Harrell, transcriber, *Savannah Courier*.

board to, which indicated, as Tim Smith reports: "Johnston actually died in the ravine fifty yards to the south."[100]

The "Wicker boys," which would include Alvis youngest sons, plus some of his oldest son, John W. Wicker's, oldest boys, as occupants and/or neighbors to the old cabin, use to cut firewood in their growing up years there near it, long after the battle but even into the park years. One time they saved a piece of wood containing a musket or Minnie ball imbedded in it. Eventually taken to Texas, it was placed on a plaque with a description of its history and displayed at Dallas during the 1936 Texas Centennial. Another example of, "near-the-old-cabin-history," that was taken elsewhere.

According to James Wicker's son, once again while on one of the boy's wood cutting trips into the forest near the old cabin at Shiloh, they also found a ramrod that had been shot into a tree. Ramrod was "a rod for ramming home the charge in a muzzle-loading firearm."[101] Did the muzzle-loader belong to a Rebel, since most of the Yankees had better guns and what was the outcome of any lives in a potential confrontation?

So many bullets were sent towards each other at Shiloh (including the old cabins original location, and, certainly its new one) that afterwards it was possible to find two that met in mid-air, never making their intended target. One was shown to this author by Shiloh local, Larry DeBerry, found on his neighboring property. A Confederate soldier had fired at the same time a Union soldier fired…the two missiles meeting in the middle…metal melting upon metal, falling harmlessly to the ground, failing to kill their intended victims.

---

[100] Smith, *The Untold Story of Shiloh*, 35.
[101] *Dictionary and Thesaurus - Merriam-Webster Online*.

Chapter 11: The New Century In 1900, The Census And Tenants...

Although, as stated earlier, there is no 1890 census today for us to read, however, it did initially record the continuing marriages, life's and deaths, of families, including those on or near the old cabin's land. On January 1st, 1901, a nineteen-year-old named Sarah Arminta Wicker began keeping a daily diary, a beautiful picture window into rural "cabin" living at the turn of the century. It is pertinent to help describe life in a cabin setting. Previously, in the 1900 census, her grandfather, widower Joseph Wicker, has daughter Sarah A. living with him, still north of Snake Creek. He is known as "Grand Pap," she as "Aunt Sack."[102] Arminta and her brothers, along with their widowed mother are living nearby. The first page of her diary, transcribed as written and spelled, follows:

DIARY OF SARAH ARMINTA (WICKER) DELANEY - January 1, 1901 thru June 16, 1902

Jan. 1, 1901, Tuesday

We killed hogs. Will Hagy, Grand Pap, Aunt Sack and Uncle John came. Ma went in the kitchen for the second time since Nov. 1900.

---

[102] "Diary of Sarah Arminta Wicker Delaney, January 1, 1901-June 16, 1902," transcribed copy courtesy of Mildred Blount, Savannah, TN.

Jan. 2, 1901, Wednesday

Aunt Kate and myself cooked up the lard and sausage. Lee went to Crump and got a barrel of Sault. I went to Grand Paps. Aunt Sallie came and brought a bucket of soap home. Henry come and got the sausage mill. Enos and Frank are going to school to Mr. Osborn Barlow.

Jan. 3, 1901, Thursday

I washed, Enos and Frank went to school Lee went to Grand Paps. Uncle John come. Him and Lee, Osborn and Calvin went to the Savannah bottom hunting tonight.

Jan. 4, 1901, Friday

I spun Ma some knitting thread, Enos and Frank went to school, Calvin come this evening to get some Laudanum to put in his mouth where he had a tooth pulled.

Jan. 5, 1901, Saturday

I ironed and washed off the kitchen floor, Aunt Kate cooked the hogs heads and feet and made Sause out of them. Lee, Enos and Frank got wood till dinner. This evening Lee went to Adamsville, Enos and Frank hawled the wood. Mr. Alonzo Blanton came this evening to buy a mule.

Jan. 6, 1901, Sunday

Henry come and we all went to Sunday School except Lee he went to Grand Paps. This evening Henry came by going to New Hope. Cletus Finger came and spent the evening with me. Osborn went to Adamsville. Frank went to Martins. Henry stopped and invited us to the singing at Mr. Kierleys tonight, as he went home.

Jan. 7, 1901, Monday

I fixed one of my dresses Aunt Kate spun some knitting thread, Lee helped Mr. Lawder get wood. Osborn hawled wood for Martin- Frank went to school- Enos stayed home with a bad cold.

Jan. 8, 1901, Tuesday

I spun Ma some knitting thread. Lee went to town and got Enos some medicine, then went to the Church and paid his and Ma's tax. Frank went to school. Osborn went and cut cord wood for Mr. Tom Phillips. I went to Aunt Sallie McDaniels...

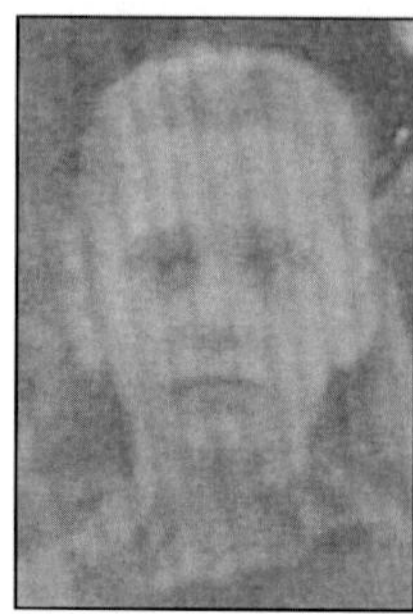

Sarah Arminta Wicker, circa 1894, about age 13.
Courtesy of Mildred Blount.

Her diary is like an old almanac. One can read it and know when to plant, what 'medicaments' to take for what ails you, what time of year to kill hogs, or pick fruit. Unfortunately it is too long to include in this work as even an appendix. Perhaps it shall be addressed at another time in future writing. In the meantime, it tells more to know.

Other entries in her diary speak like a weather report for the old cabin at Shiloh. She tells of rain, sleet and snow at various times over her year and a half of diary keeping.

Earlier in this work in the memoirs of Emmet Strawn, born a year later than Sarah but in the same Snake Creek area, he mentions "log rolling," which undoubtedly occurred around the old cabin at both its original and latest location. Following is an entry from her diary regarding that job, apparently not popular with all young people. The first three mentioned are her brothers, two older and one younger. The next are friends and "suitors" to the nineteen-year-old Sarah Arminta. They, apparently, choosing women over work:

Feb 11, 1901. Monday

> *Mr. John McDaniel stopped this morning and asked Lee, Osborne and Enos to help him log roll this evening. Cletus and Chester passed on the log rolling this evening.*

In other entries from her diary, the young people were preparing for an outing in a wagon to Shiloh. Based on the date, it's not known if a special occasion was occurring that Sunday, as there was later, which she attended and will be reported. Here are her entries:

June 3, 1901. Monday

> *Lee is gone tonight to see if Mabel Duren will go with him to Shiloh next Sunday in a wagon.*

June 4, 1901. Tuesday

> *Lee is gone to New Hope tonight to see Jas. L. and Cletus and fix up their trip to Shiloh Sunday.*

June 8, 1901. Saturday

> *I swept the yard this morning and prepared my dinner this evening to take to Shiloh tomorrow.*

June 9, 1901. Sunday

> *It rained this morning and we did not go to Shiloh. Lee, Mabel, James L., Elva, Cletus and I were aiming to go in a wagon.*

Would they have visited the old cabin if they had made it there? In speaking of it, the research paper from 1934 indicates, "The 'War Cabin' has not been used as a dwelling, except for two brief intervals for several years…" It is possible this author has discovered those two times with the following information:

In early 2007, this author met the then 93-year-old Sallie White of Adamsville, Tennessee. She knows a great deal of the history in that area. She reported that one of her former neighbors, a Mr. Hendrix, had told her his mother, whose maiden name was Hoover, had lived in the cabin at the park at one time. A check of the 1900 census in Hardin County showed a Hoover family there, quite possibly them. Now whether she lived there then or later is unknown. Hoover's are still in Hardin in 1910.

As reported earlier, Dr. Ronnie Fullwood's grandmother, Dora (Patrick) Cody, lived in the cabin as seven-year-old Dora Patrick in 1905. She told a story of how her father was a sleepwalker and that one night he fell out the cabin window by the fireplace and barely missed a double-bladed ax. It was stuck in a block of wood, used to split logs to burn in the cabin's fireplace. Her parents were tenants in the park at that time. They are in that district in the Hardin County 1900 census but are in nearby McNairy County by 1910.

If John W. Wicker still lived on the property during either of these above times mentioned, then it reinforces that he would have been in his own cabin on the property. If the park's 1895 era picture is to be accepted, then this also reinforces that John and family lived in another cabin there. He and wife Martha had two of their seven children by the time the land was bought. In spite of what we would consider today as a hazard, those children probably played around and in the old dilapidated cabin, although initially in 1885 it may have still been usable by them for whatever purpose. As indicated earlier, if John was a tenant on the property since his marriage in January of 1878, they may have lived in it while building a better cabin in which they actually raised their children.

After purchasing the land it was on in 1897, the War

Department had the old cabin made livable, even adding the window next to the chimney for ease of getting firewood into the home, a fairly standard feature for the day. This was done at least by 1905, for tenancy.

The War Department did not have the preservation and restoration rules the NPS has today, as followed by Ranger Tom Parson in 2003, thus the added window. They were apparently willing and maybe even looking to have tenants occupy the rehabbed dwelling for park incomes sake. Even later in 1962, the NPS didn't have as strict a guideline either as they added the porch, which was removed in 2003 to adhere to new NPS rules.

Description of Life in the 1910-1920's Era at the Park and Cabin.

Cabins are about people and to tell a cabin's history is to tell the families history that lived in or around any cabin, or as now, specifically, the old cabin in the park. Therefore, the following are excerpts from memoirs written by Miriam (Bell) Holden in 1982. She was born in the park on September 21, 1913. It should be noted that the references to "Grandma Bell" and her orchard is not Widow Sarah Bell or her now famous Peach Orchard, but the next generation removed. However, all are living in the park, with the old cabin nearby, where remembrances and experiences could easily occur. Further clarification or information put together by this author is inserted in italicized brackets:

Memories Memories – 1913 –

…We had to borrow horse and buggy or wagon from Grandma Bell [Matilda Catherine (Hagy) Bell] for our trips, or walk. Papa [Charles S. Bell] did have a bicycle he rode to work [at the park] and he would ride us children when we were

small.

Kathleen, my oldest sister [born December 1910], and I were born in a four room house back of Grandma Bell's orchard. I think this house was built for Papa and Mama [Mary Rosaline Sowell] when they were married [before October 1909]. It had two bedrooms and the kitchen had a dining area in it. One room was a junk room or a storage room. One bedroom was our sitting room — I believe we called it then. The junk room had a trap door in the floor where you could go down in the cellar. It was not concrete — just a dirt floor and walls where we could store fruit and other things to keep them from freezing but one of its main purposes was in case of a cyclone. A cyclone had hit Shiloh and Pittsburg Landing [October 14, 1909[103]*] just a short time before my parents were married and several were killed. None of the Bell or Sowell families were killed. It blew the roof from Grandma Bell's house but no one was hurt there. Their house was log, covered with weatherboard and the log may have been what saved them. It seems that everybody had a storm cellar after that. Several were killed in the cyclone.*

The Wicker/George cabin or the 'War Cabin' as it was called then, apparently survived this "cyclone," or tornado, as no reports within the park indicate otherwise. Continuing on now with Miriam's memoirs…

Grandma had a big orchard. We had a path up through the orchard to Grandma's house. There was a lane down beside the orchard for buggy's and wagons. There was a white picket fence around our yard.
We didn't have running water. There was a well in the yard and we went outside to the toilet.

I remember Papa worked at the Shiloh Park headquarters [laborer there per the 1910 census] which was

[103] Smith, *This Great Battlefield of Shiloh*, 107.

about 1/2 mile by way of a path and about a mile around the road. I guess he went around the road on his bicycle as there was a log to walk across a stream on the way by path. We children chose the short way when we went to the store for Mamma or Grandma. We took eggs to sell and sometimes we got to spend a nickel. The post office was in the store, too, and we went there for the mail. The paper came by mail and we loved the trip for the mail.

There were roses in the yard. We had a vegetable garden with Grandma. The orchard had lots of apple, peach, pear, cherry trees and I remember one quince tree. The fruit from this was used for preserves, which were real good.

They canned the apples, peaches, cherries and pears and they also dried large quantities of apples and peaches. They had large pieces of roofing tin to lay the fruit on to dry. They put these pieces of roofing on carpenter horses and set them in the sun. At night they were brought in the back porch to keep them from getting damp. They were put out several days in the sun and then heated slightly in the oven in case insects were in them and then they were stored in a heavy cloth sack called a meal sack. The apples and peaches made mighty good fried pies and dumplings in the winter.

There were very few things our grandparents had to get from the grocery. They had hogs they killed, calves and goats and chickens. They had no ice box or refrigerators, then, in the country. We were 20 miles from town so if beef and goats were killed in the summer it was divided out among neighbors, friends and family to eat before it spoiled. Chickens were killed on the day they were used.

We had our own cow for milk and butter. Milk had to be kept in the cellar to keep it cool or set in the well bucket and let down in the well. Some people had a spring near the house where they kept milk and butter and other things cool. They built little houses over a stream of the spring and had an opening at each end for the water to run through. You sat your milk bucket in the water and weighted it down with a clean rock. Butter, vegetables and other things were usually set in buckets and put the lid on and weight them down with a rock. The little spring house had a hinged lid on it to raise up and get your food out. These houses protected your food from animals getting into it.

My grandparents and mother carried their food to the cellar to keep it cool. Grandma Bell had a nice concrete cellar but you had to go outside to get to it. There were outside steps and a door that opened outside. Aunt Ethel said she made a million trips a day it seemed to the cellar. You had to go get the food for a meal then take it back after the meal. Nobody had to jog or take walks then. You got your exercise doing the chores.

I'm not sure when we moved from the little house but Kathleen and I were small. We moved to a house in the middle of Shiloh Park that had the telephone switchboard in it. My Aunt Maude Sowell, Mamma's youngest sister, was the switchboard operator in the day time. Mamma and Papa took care of it at night. There were only emergency calls at night.

All the Shiloh Park employees had phones in their homes. Phones in the country were otherwise rare.

Our closest neighbors at this place were Mamma's brother and his family...Another close neighbor was the Superintendent of the Park and his family [Delong Rice[104]]. Grandma Sowell [Melissa (Jones) Sowell] lived about a mile away. They lived in the house where Mamma and her brothers and sisters grew up. The Park took over this home and they were allowed to live on there as Grandpa Sowell [James White Sowell] was an employee. The house had a front and back porch. On the back porch, which was real big, was the well where they got their water. This was a luxury as they didn't have to go out in the rain and snow, etc.

I don't know how long we lived at the "Switchboard

---

[104] Smith, *This Great Battlefield of Shiloh*, 122.

House" as we called it. I do remember one real big snow - 18 inches - that fell while we were there. Grandpa came with a sled behind a mule and drug out paths to the well, toilet, barn, chicken house and mail box.

Upon interviewing Miriam, the "Switchboard House" was located closer to the northwest end of the Sunken Road but still not far from the old cabin at the southeast end. After a period of time, Miriam and her family moved to Arkansas, then back to Shiloh, Tennessee, then Corinth, Mississippi. They could not be found in the 1920 census in either place but her story continues within that era:

Charles [Bell, her brother] was born at Shiloh [about 1923] after we came back from Arkansas...[then to] Corinth, Mississippi which is just across the line from the Shiloh area. We lived in Corinth until I finished the 8th grade. We lived across from the National Cemetery...We didn't have a car but Papa would get somebody to drive us all to Shiloh on occasions, especially at Christmas time. The grandmothers and Aunt Ethel would make big preparations for our coming. There would be lots of cakes, pies, homemade candy and all kind of goodies. There was a big smoke house full of hams, sausage and side meat.

The smoke house at Grandma Bell's was big with a floored attic. I remember lots of Civil War relics in there. There were bullets, bayonets, guns and cannon balls, etc. which were picked up on Shiloh battlefield [Some, perhaps near the old cabin]. Grandpa Bell [James William Bell] fought in the Civil War. I remember his gun and uniform. Oh how I wish we had saved some of these. There were 2 big barns at Grandma Bell's.

Uncle Braz, who never married, lived there with Grandma and he had beautiful horses and mules. I especially remember his big black mules. He used a currycomb on them and they were so black and shiny. They and all his livestock were well fed and cared for... Uncle Braz had a mussel camp on the place, down by the Tennessee River. He had several rowboats that went out every day that it was suitable and caught mussels.

They had a place where they cooked these so they could get the shells open and the meat out. I don't know what they did with the meat but the shells were loaded on a barge that came by. They were shipped to a factory to make pearl buttons and buckles.[105]

And so life was, around the park and the old cabin, on the west side of the Tennessee River after the turn of the century and into the 1920's. According to Miriam, she remembers seeing and passing by the old cabin at times, but never in her early memory recalls tenants there. However, when the George's bought, moved and lived in it several years, it became part of the Bell-George family and thus a part of Miriam (Bell) Holden's history, as well as the Wicker's.

From Youngest Cabin Occupant in 1849, to a 1910 Neighbor...

Another park occupant, once again by 1910, was Elzina (Wicker) Green. Initially she was the youngest occupant, at age six, of the original cabin her father Lewis built for the family by 1849. After that she also will have witnessed, and know about, that original cabin being moved to the neighbor's, the Georges, after the battle in 1862.

It was the Shiloh battle itself that first caused Elzina and husband Dennis to cross paths, near Owl Creek, with her

[105] Miriam Bell Holden, "Memories, Memories – 1913 –," quoted in Stokes, "The Bell Family at Shiloh."

and the three children possibly coming from the old cabin, or a neighboring one. His regiment was recruited from McNairy, and Dennis went on to war but obviously never forgot the chance encounter before the battle. Appomattox occurred in April 1865 and Dennis indicated his unit disbanded "at Corinth, Mississippi." Before continuing to McNairy, did the twice-wounded Sergeant Green come straight up the road from Corinth into Tennessee and Shiloh battleground, past the old cabin, to next door "Wicker Field," and find the face that fueled him every waking day in the war?

Apparently so, and he must have returned often, as they were married within two months. Perhaps while coming to court Elzina, he found her visiting teenaged Sarah George, living next door in the old Wicker cabin with her family. Elzina, initially living next door to the old cabin from 1865, by 1900 she had moved to McNairy County next door to Hardin, as already indicated. Her husband died in 1906.

So by the 1910 census, Elzina was back in Hardin County with son, Hoyt, living next to another son, Delzert, and his family. Also in Hardin were son, Monsel, and his family. In an irony of all ironies, all three of Dennis and Elzina's sons censused above were…working at Shiloh National Military Park. Did she tell them the cabin history? Nine men in all on the two census pages recorded with the Green's, were working there, including Elzina's census neighbor, Park Commissioner David Reed. One wonders, how many of those men worked at some time on the old cabin, took their lunch in its shade, or just passed by on the way to or from work? Park development was in full swing.

In speaking of that park development, this author was told of one of Elzina's relatives, a Wicker, that had a team of mules and helped unload monuments from the ships on the Tennessee River at Pittsburg Landing and pull statues into place in the park. Again, some of this activity passing by and occurring around the old cabin throughout those developmental years. That Wicker probably knew the family connection to the old cabin and may have visited it, if not helping place cannons and monuments in the fields nearby.

Elzina died in 1929...the last known to do so of the original cabin occupants.

What Economic Effect Did the Park Have on the County and the Cabin?

In August of 1930, two months before the beginning of the Great Depression and three years before even the National Park Service took over operation of Shiloh National Military Park, a college Master's degree thesis was written about the economic and social development of Hardin County after 1865. The writer was none other than Miss Lear Pearl Durbin, local teacher at Shiloh School, and, future CWA writer at the park. In her paper, she writes this portion on the park itself (with this author's bracket inserts):

In 1895 the Shiloh Battlefield was occupied by citizens who lived in their own homes and cultivated a great part of the land. When this property was purchased, some of these people remained in their houses and worked for the Government. Others left the park boundaries, were unable to locate a home that was satisfactory at another place, are old now, and will never have a residence again that they can call their own.

The complete preservation of the battlefield could not be maintained if the soil were cultivated, therefore, a great farming area is removed from the County and a great amount of valuable timber can never be cut. Not only is this true, but the County receives no revenue from the territory which the Park includes.

Thus when the inconvenience of people who gave up their homes, and the removing of a source of revenue are considered, the Shiloh National Military Park seems to be an economic and social disadvantage to Hardin County, but, after weighing the opportunities for advancement it has given the people, one may be safe in saying that this protected area been a great asset to this isolated section.

The National Government has spent...dollars on the Shiloh National Military Park. The citizens of the community received a great part of this...since they were the laborers [some living in or near the old cabin] who did the work as the plans were being executed. The government has furnished employment for many people who at times of the year would otherwise have been idle. In addition...the state and civic organizations have expended...dollars. The driveways through the Park were the first graded roads in the County, and they served as a great help in linking up the public highways at least when this building project was begun...The Park also serves as a great advertisement for this section...

Socially we may say that in bringing so many people [visitors] into the County, this Park has been the means of getting its residents a general knowledge of the outside world, that they have necessarily been affected by the social contact, and all of this influence has been an educational force in their lives. The charm and beauty which characterizes the place cannot help but have a great aesthetic value for the people who could not have received this influence from any other place.[106]

Thus ends her thesis excerpt. The area around the old cabin was farmed both before the battle and afterwards even through some park tenancy times in the early 1900's. Nowadays, certain open field areas, including ones near the old

---

[106] Lear Pearl Durbin, "Economic and Social Development of Hardin County Tennessee Since 1865" (thesis for Master of Arts in History degree, George Peabody College for Teachers, August 1930), 70-72. Copy courtesy of Connie Lewis, Assistant Director/Reference & Genealogy, Hardin County Public Library.

cabin, are leased out by the park to grow hay to harvest. One of the lessees, pioneer Shiloh family member, Dr. Ronnie Fullwood (who rents "Wicker Field" next to the old cabin), reports on this aspect:

The land is quite poor so there is not much production of hay especially with the low rainfall in recent years. I pay only [a few] dollars per acre to rent for hay and we are required to keep the soil fertilized and limed, per soil test. This money goes to the National Park Service so the county actually receives no money as far as I know. Of course, since it is Federal property it is exempt from county land taxes, etc.[107]

Obviously this is limited to a scale covering the open fields currently maintained as part of the battleground where monuments reside today. One can agree with Miss Durbin that while agricultural areas have been taken out of potential operation because of the park, including those about the old cabin, the social and other economic benefits outweighs these agrarian losses.

When historical events occur, such as the battle in 1862, it changes conditions, lives and the course of human behavior. The existence and direction of pre-battle life was interrupted and then allowed to settle in again for the next thirty years or so. Then another event occurred; the establishment of the Shiloh National Military Park in 1894 and it brought the subsequent salvation of the old cabin. What the battle took away from private occupants, to some degree the park itself has restored. Over the years it has offered jobs to citizens in the area, and still does today, and its visitors have brought with them some economic trade. The resiliency of humanity and the resolve to adapt and continue on are by-products of the pioneers that settled this area to start

[107] Dr. Ronnie Fullwood, land lessee, Shiloh Nat. Mil. Park, e-mail message to author, September 7, 2007.

with…many years ago. This includes those, and all others, eventually involved in the old cabins life, over time.

Also in 1930, in the census, former cabin land owner, John W. Wicker, although the cabin land was then owned by the USA, was still living either on that land, or, on next-door Wicker Field. His son, Herbert, at that time, was reported as working at the National Cemetery there at Pittsburg Landing. Both of these indications led in part to the upcoming 1934 interview of John by Miss Durbin for her research paper. Since it is not known when John W. Wicker died, he may have lived on that land for some years yet.

Chapter 12:
Changing Of The Guard – A New Era For The Cabin In 1933

In 1933 there came a changing of the guard at Shiloh National Military Park. The National Park Service took over for the War Department and further changes would begin for the old cabin. It was the time of our Great Depression.

Because of Roosevelt's, New Deal, Shiloh ironically reaped benefits during a period in which most of America was drowning in economic crisis. Many government agencies sent workers to the park, such as two Civilian Conservation Corps camps, as well as Works Progress Administration [WPA] workers writing histories of various aspects of the battlefield.[108]

One offshoot of the WPA, of many depression era programs, the Civil Works Administration, will specifically benefit the cabin's history of which is reported:

An examination of the activities of the CWA under the jurisdiction of the National Park Service, which were carried out between November 28, 1933, and April 28, 1934, serves as a good example of how a New Deal emergency public works

[108] Smith, *This Great Battlefield of Shiloh*, 127.

program supplemented the ongoing implementation of the National Park Service program.

To assist in the administration of this program the Park Service director was requested to organize and supervise the work of as many workers as could be used profitably in connection with work in the national parks and monuments...On November 28 the Park Service civil works program was approved, and a total of 14,031 workers was authorized.

The CWA program under the jurisdiction of the Park Service employed a total of 12,942 men and 192 women prior to its abolition and performed a number of park development projects...Other types of work in the parks included...remodeling old buildings...preservation of historic and prehistoric areas and structures...[109]

Wickers are not yet through with their input into the old cabin's history. As stated, a grandson of Lewis Wicker and himself a former owner of the cabin, John W. Wicker, will be interviewed by the 1934 CWA research writer, Miss Lear Durbin. Since Miss Durbin is a local, born there in 1884, she not only witnessed the initial preservation of the cabin, but knew John W. Wicker when he told her its history. As indicated, he was living on Wicker Field, or, cabin land in 1930, and apparently still there by the 1934 interview.

Miss Durbin must have finished her paper before April 28 in 1934. She is one of only 192 CWA women, as reported, and was a local public school teacher by age 26, in the 1910 census, and, later teaching at Shiloh school by 1917, as the following excerpt confirms:

[109] Harlan D. Unrau and G. Frank Williss, *Administrative History: Expansion of the National Park Service in the 1930s* (September 1983), "Chapter Three: Impact of the New Deal on the National Park Service," http://www.nps.gov/history/history/online_books/unrau-williss/adhi3c.htm.

In 1917, with both the school and church buildings in Shiloh in a deteriorating state, a drive was started in the community to raise funds to build new structures. Lear Durbin (a school teacher at the time) and Katie Barnett (wife of Herb Barnett) spearheaded the drive to raise funds for a new school. Box suppers, cake walks and even production plays at the school were all used to raise funds.[110]

A photocopy was obtained of Miss Durbin's typed research paper that is in Shiloh National Military Park records and was computer transcribed for input purposes here. Following, between this author's continuing narratives, are excerpts from that paper with its own footnotes denoted, and, bracketed inserts to clarify or correct:

The "War Cabin" – Its History And Proposed Construction

History of the "War Cabin."

In 1862 many homes dotted the area which became the Battlefield of Shiloh, and it seems strange that only one should remain through the intervening years to be designated as the "War Cabin," for in truth this [the] original house [on this site] was destroyed during the terrible conflict while several other buildings withstood the storm of shot and shell.

The following history, however, which has been collected from interviews of citizens who remember conditions as they existed at that time, gives us all the information that can be obtained concerning this re-nowned [sic] house.

Mrs. [Sarah] Bell owned property in this section of the battlefield and lived in a house which stood where the present one is located on the road between the Bloody Pond and

---

[110] Fullwood, *Shiloh's House of Peace*, 67.

Johnston's Monument. Her daughter [Nancy] married Manse George and the mother gave them several acres of land on which was located a house at the [present] "War Cabin" site.

When the battle opened on that eventful morning, Mr. George's family were compelled to move as other people within the range of the guns, were forced to do. But it was around his home that a part of the most severe fighting was waged.

The fire from the guns was so intense that the timber nearly became ignited, and, as the beautiful peach blossoms in the orchard on the south were being cut from the twigs by the flying bullets, Johnston is reported to have said they were falling like snow. As soon as it was possible for Mr. George to return to his residence after the battle, he found it in ruins.

But several years before the War Between the States [November 6, 1848], Louis [sic-'Lewis'] Wicker had bought land [400 acres in Entry #1723] in the Pittsburg area and had built a house near the place on which the Tilghman home was located later [deeds show at today's park entrance]. This dwelling stood through the battle, and sometime after the conflict, Manse George purchased it, and moved it to the site which his former residence occupied, thus building what in future years was to be known as the "War Cabin." With the exception of a few logs which have replaced old ones because of decay all of the logs in this house are the battle scarred ones of the Louis [sic-'Lewis'] Wicker home.

The above paragraph was reported earlier but repeated here to allow the historical continuity of the research paper. The research writer goes on to say:

This property has been owned by several different people since Mr. George built [sic - 'moved'] the house...

Four ownerships have been documented after the George's left for Texas, apparently as early as 1871. One was a W. M. Cunningham who acquired it from the Bell family heirs in that year in Texas. He sold to O. H. P. Cantrell in Hardin County a month later and the next ownership was John W. Wicker, as follows, who sold it in 1896 to Samuel Chambers, who in turn sold to the USA for the park in 1897.

...but when the government bought it after the battlefield had been established as a National Military Park, the homestead, which included the residence and sixty-five acres of land, belonged to John [W.] Wicker, a grandson of Louis [sic-'Lewis'] Wicker.[111]

The acreage listed above is correct, based on deed research. However, the aforementioned Samuel Chambers actually deeded it to the USA in 1897, as stated. He sold several pieces (at least six) to the USA and he may have become or been something of a real estate entrepreneur for his day, seeing what was coming with park establishment in 1894 and development, and buying up future needed park lands to in turn sell them to the War Department. Chambers did own "543.42 acres," the most any one person sold.[112]

The "War Cabin" has not been used as a dwelling, except for two brief intervals for several years, but it has undergone repairs during the period in which it was occupied.

The "two brief intervals" should include the two previously indicated occupants and as to the "for several years" reference, one can guess it goes back into the 1920's if not further. It would appear that at the time of the National Park Service taking over for the War Department in 1933, the "War Cabin" was not occupied. From the picture below taken in 1931 of visitors in their Sunday finery, there were weeds in

[111] Wicker, John, Personal Interview, 1934, footnoted by Lear Durbin, "The 'War Cabin'– It's History and Proposed Construction" (Research paper, SNMP, April, 1934), author Duane Helweg's italicized brackets.
[112] Smith, *This Great Battlefield of Shiloh*, 40.

front and the chimney top was gone.

Unknown 1931 park visitors.
Courtesy of Shiloh National Military Park (SNMP)

Even the War Department was apparently showing it as a tour stop by 1927.[113] It would then be the National Park Service who eventually identified it as it is today on their message board at the tour stop, the "Manse George Cabin."

Most of the "Present Condition of the Cabin" from the research paper was reported earlier in this history. However, the last sentences in the continuance to follow indicate an attempt to "restore" the cabin a "few years ago." This could be referring to the War Department's restoration in the late 1890's which would have allowed subsequent tenant occupancy, or, even later during their era. We can know the NPS began a restoration by at least 1934 based on what was printed and attached to the back of a park picture of that date. It stated, "Work is currently taking place…on the William Manse George Cabin. Many features of the structure have deteriorated

[113] Smith, *This Great Battlefield of Shiloh*, 123-124.

over time. The park will restore those features to preserve and interpret the importance of the antebellum log structure."

1934 photo with printed caption on the back side. Courtesy of SNMP.

That "importance" was initially reflected by the War Department in the mid-1890's when they chose to preserve the old cabin and now by the NPS when they took over. It is important for those who visit the park today to realize that more than just an historic battle took place there. People were living there throughout the battlefield, and although "fields" so named on maps or in historical writings are reminders, the Shiloh Church and Cemetery, and the old cabin with its Peach Orchard neighbor, are the lone reminders of that fact within the park. To not have and recognize all of these would imply visually to the park visitor that the battle was fought basically in forest and meadow, which was not the case. There were soldiers camped around homes and on their private fields.

As stated above, under "Present Condition of the Cabin," most of that portion was earlier reported as the history of actually how it may have been originally built by the Wickers.

Here continues input from that section:

...A few years ago there was a movement to restore this cabin to its original construction. The decayed logs, which included some of those that contained holes for the warping board, were removed and new ones were put in their place. The stick-and-dirt chimney was partly rebuilt, but the plan was abandoned when very little more than the framing of the fireplace was finished. This is its condition now.

The type of architecture and finishing materials used in either Mr. George's home which was destroyed during the battle or at that of Mr. Wicker which replaced it is not known but since Mr. Wicker owned a considerable amount of property [400 acres] and had a large family [eleven], it is supposed that his home was a large one and well built for that day. The "War Cabin" may represent only a part of the former dwelling.

This idea of Wicker having built more than what is suggested as being only a "part of the former dwelling" has been covered earlier. Having a wife, seven sons, four daughters and a slave in 1848, he may well have constructed more than one building, including a separate kitchen cooking facility and slave quarter cabin, or even attachments.

In the following, Miss Durbin, the CWA writer, reads literature on, studies local dwellings of the era and conducts interviews of local people to gain building and furniture insight to report on. There are terms used in some descriptions, the definitions of which this author was unaware. Should the reader also need help understanding these, they are included under a "Definition of Terms" in **Appendix #2** as indicated earlier.

<u>Other Cabins of the Period.</u>

The only way to arrive at a conclusion concerning the condition of Mr. George's house at the time of the battle is to read the literature that has been written on living conditions in the South during the pre-war time, to study the dwellings of that period which still stand in this community, and to interview people who remember the architecture and furnishings of homes in those days. Since this family owned its home, the house, it is believed, represented in its construction and furnishings the average home in this section. All of these buildings were simple in structure, being erected of hewed logs, but there was a choice to be made in selecting the finishing materials.

Today's sills at each bottom corner, about twelve inches square. Author's photo 2007.

"The popular size of a house was eighteen feet wide and twenty feet long. To begin at the foundation of a house, the

first thing ordered were two side sills, placed on blocks of wood or pillars of stone. The sills were twenty feet long and usually eighteen inches square. Sometimes this size was reduced to twelve or fourteen inches square, but it was generally considered unsafe to use a smaller sill than eighteen inches..."

"The sleepers, which rested on the sills and supported the floor, were round logs about twelve inches in diameter. They hewed to a line on top, with a face from three to five inches wide, and made to fit the sills by a flat notch at each end."

"The floors were made of either puncheons or dirt. It was no unusual thing to leave out the sleepers and use the ground for a floor. In fact, when a man was able to have two houses, the one used for a kitchen and dining room almost invariably had a dirt floor."

"Puncheons were broad pieces of timber, split from pine or poplar trees, with maul and wedge, and hewed to a smooth surface on one side with a broad-ax. They were usually six feet long, from three to four inches thick, and from ten to twenty inches wide. They were trimmed at each end with an ax till they fit neatly and solidly on the sleepers, smooth side up, and were heavy enough to remain in position when once properly put down, without being

Man with maul and wedge (or froe), as described[114]

[114] "Department of Conservation Photograph Collection, 1937-1976," *Tennessee Virtual Archive (TeVA).*

fastened in any way."

"Those old puncheon floors were neither air tight nor ornamental. The edges of each puncheon were hewed to a line with a broad-ax, and when the cracks between them did not measure over an inch in width at any place, the floor was considered well jointed."

Duane Helweg inside cabin showing floor, fireplace, window and stair step (left). 2006 photo by the author's wife.

"Before nails came into general use, the cracks between the logs in the walls were 'chinked' with small blocks of wood split for the purpose, and 'daubed' with mud made from red clay and plastered by hand. The process of daubing a house was very simple. A man stood near the crack and threw the soft mud against the chink by handfuls with sufficient force to make it stick fast. When a crack was thus 'daubed' the full length of the house, he would press the ends of his fingers against the "daubing" after the manner of the brick-layers trowel, and walked rapidly along the house so as to draw his fingers over the full length of the crack, thus smoothing down

the 'daubing.'...

To chink a house was to put blocks of wood, called 'chinking' in the cracks, and to 'daub' it was to put mud on the "chinking" in the manner described."

"...After nails came into use the cracks in the houses were stopped by nailing clapboards over them. The roof of every house was made of clapboards. The clapboard was simply a piece of riven timber, usually oak, four feet long, from four to six inches wide and about a half inch thick. At a later day clapboards were made three feet long and, in some cases, as short as two feet..."

"The first improvement we made upon those rude huts, in the architecture of our homes, was to build hewed log houses. We used whip-sawed lumber for floors and put on clapboard roofs with rafters, lathing and nails. We made the doors of whip-sawed lumber, hung them with iron hinges made in the blacksmith shop, and put 'store bought' locks and brass knobs on them. We put joists in the house, and laid a loft, and built stairs of whip-sawed lumber. We daubed the cracks with mortar, made of lime and sand, smoothed them over with a trowel, while the mortar was soft, and neatly white-washed them when thoroughly dry. We built stone chimneys, put in glass windows, talked about the great and rapid improvements the world was making, and began to look for the dawn of the 'Millennium.'"[115]

These homes were heated by means of an open fireplace. The chimneys were built by brick and many times of stick-and-dirt.

"The heating apparatus was a large open fire-place in one end of the cabin. Ordinarily such a fireplace was about five feet long, two feet deep, and five feet high. The chimney was built of wood and lined with mud, made of red clay. When

---

[115] Srygley, *Seventy Years in Dixie*, Nashville 1893, pp. 131-135, footnoted by Lear Durbin, "The 'War Cabin'– It's History and Proposed Construction" (Research paper, SNMP, April, 1934).

the mud got thoroughly dry it was as hard as brick. The fire-place was lined–bottom back and sides– with large flat rocks. The top of the fire-place, in front, was simply the first log of the cabin wall, above the opening cut out of the fire-place. This log had to be high enough not to catch fire, and hence was fully five feet above the level of the hearth, or bottom of the fire-place.

The funnel of the chimney "was simply a pan about two feet square, built of small sticks. Sometimes the sticks were around poles with a flat notch at each end, so that they would fit together steadily, but oftener they were narrower riven slats, about an inch thick by two inches wide."[116]

The architecture of the pre-war in Hardin County is revealed in a house on the Hindman road, not much of a dwelling now remains, one room and hall being entirely gone, and the other room moved, but with this evidence together with the knowledge of citizens who remember the house in its original construction, it is possible to get a very complete description of the structure when it was first built.

Hindman Road is about five miles south of the park, "as the crow flies," so to speak. It was between Lick Creek and Watkins Road on the north side of today's Highway 57. As indicated by the following, this house was "raised" about the same time as the old cabin.

This house was raised on entered land about 1850. It is constructed of very large logs so well hewed that they look as if they were planed. The joist and rafters are hewed in the same way. The floor was puncheon which was made of logs hewed on one side as smooth as dressed plank. This puncheon was notched underneath to fit over the sleepers, and all of this work was so carefully done that the floor was very much like a

[116] Ibid, p. 138.

tongue-and-grooved one. No nails were needed for this floor, for its weight and careful laying kept it in place. Wooden pins were used for nailing the rafters and framing the fireplace. The logs of this house are joined by the square notch.

There were two large rooms to this house connected by about an eight foot hall. The stairway was in this hall, and an upstairs floor of plank was laid over each of the rooms. This second story was unceiled.

The chimney of this house was made of sand rock which is abundant in this community. The fireplace was finished with this material and the hearth was built from the ground to the floor level with this rock which was held in place with a clay daub, and given a perfectly smooth finish with this plaster. Two iron bars held the arch and a mantel framed the fireplace.[117]

The Hindman home, which is located near the foot of Hindman Hill, is another pre-war dwelling which dates back about seventy-seven years. This house has been enlarged since the war, but the north room is the original structure. It is made of hewed logs, and the walls are chinked and daubed. This plaster, however, has been redone in recent years. The floor is laid of plank which are so well fitted that it is difficult to see that they're not tongued-and-grooved. They are about six inches wide. There is an upstairs floor laid of plank on hewed joists. This second story is unceiled. The staircase makes a turn as it extends to the upper floor. It is boxed in such a way as to enclose a low closet. The doors of this house are made of planed plank, and the door openings are framed with the plank in very much the same way as are the houses of to-day.

Picture number one in the leaflet shows a corner of a pre-war house which is located at the approach to Stantonville on Highway fifty-seven.

---

[117] Wicker, John, Personal Interview 1934, footnoted by Lear Durbin, "The 'War Cabin'– It's History and Proposed Construction."
Harrison, Will, Personal Interview 1934, footnoted by Lear Durbin, "The 'War Cabin'– It's History and Proposed Construction."

Obviously the writer had prepared a leaflet (which the park today does not have), to go with this research paper showing photos of probably not only those houses mentioned herein, but possibly some of the 'War Cabin' itself. Those homes, such as the above, are not on park lands. Photography was part of some WPA programs. Continuing now:

This property has been owned by Mrs. Paralee McDaniel since 1883. Her friends who lived before the War Between the States have given her evidence that leads her to believe her house is about one hundred years old.

The dwelling is constructed of hewed logs and comprises two large rooms as connected by a very wide open hall. Traces of the chinking and daubing can yet be seen. The floors are laid of plank well fitted together. One room and the hall were not originally ceiled overhead. The other room has an upstairs floor laid of plank. This second story room is unceiled. The first roof of this house is said to have been of cypress shingles put on with nails. The doors are well made of hand planed plank, hung on iron hinges, and fastened with iron latches. The chimneys are of brick and have stood in an excellent state of preservation until of recent years. There are five windows in this house which were originally fitted with twelve pane sashes, but some of them now are closed with wooden shutters.

Other houses near Stantonville which date earlier than 1840 have been studied, but they reveal about the same type of architecture as those which have been described.

Many of the homes in the Shiloh community had puncheon floors and stick-and-dirt chimneys.[118] *The puncheon in these homes were usually made by hewing one side of a log very smooth.*

---

[118] Smith, Mrs. Mary, Personal Interview, 1934, footnoted by Lear Durbin, "The 'War Cabin'– It's History and Proposed Construction."

There are no stick-and-dirt chimneys standing to give evidence of their mode of construction and the pre-war period, but Srygley's description of them verifies that of citizens who remember the manner in which they were built.

The lower part of the chimney which enclosed the fireplace which usually made of logs which were fitted together somewhat like the logs of the house, but sometimes boxing for this purpose was made of plank or riven boards. Either of this wood material was used as the frame work which held the mud until it became very dry and hard. After it decayed and fell away, the chimney stood indefinitely.

April 2002 'Women in the War' demonstration showing the old (pre-2003 rehab) fireplace, the open window, and, stairs inside. Author's photo.

The fireplace was sometimes lined with native rock which was plastered with the clay, but frequently nothing but the mud was used.[119] *A frame was made for the hearth, jambs, and arch and packed with the daub. This framing was removed when the dirt became dry. Sometimes a log of the house supported the arch, but iron bars were also used for this purpose. The jambs were frequently arranged with shelves which were convenient places to set dishes for the purpose of*

[119] Fraley, M. F., Personal Interview, 1934, footnoted by Durbin.

keeping the food warm. There was also an iron bar placed behind the one which supported the arch. Its purpose was to hold the S-shaped box from which the kettle's for cooking were suspended over the fire. This bar was sometimes merely a wooden pole. If it burned another had to be inserted. This bar was usually wood if the first log of the house above the fireplace supported the arch.[120] *Many of these fireplaces contained a pole on one side nearly to the top for the purpose of inserting the handle of the grease lamp. These fireplaces were usually framed with a mantel which consisted of a plank on either side and one above the arch over which a shelf was arranged by laying a plank on small braces at the ends for support.*

Furnishings of a Cabin of the Period.

The furnishings of these houses were in keeping with the simplicity of the structure of the buildings, although the choices of materials as walnut and cherry were used for these home-made articles. "a [sic] furnished room contained, say, a bed, a few rough chairs and stools, and a log bench, a dining table and a cupboard made of rough clapboards."

The bedsteads were four posters and corded. There were no slats or springs, but cords of rope were inserted through holes that were made in their rails and crossed the length and breadth of the bedstead, making a kind of checked effect.

Here this author will convey to the reader the history of the term, "Sleep tight." The cords of rope mentioned above were made of cotton which has a stretch ability to it under weight and over time. Therefore, wooden dowels were placed within the cords at one length and one breadth on the outside of

[120] Wood, Frank, Personal Interview, 1934, footnoted by Durbin.

the bedstead. When the bed occupant's weight on the ticking mattress had stretched the cords over time, allowing all to droop to an uncomfortable position, the dowels were twisted along the two sides, creating once again a taut position to sleep on. Two such beds are inside the cabin today at the park.

A ticking filled with straw, either of millet or of the wheat plant made the mattress that was placed upon these cords and other ticking was filled with feathers and laid upon this mattress. These bedsteads were very high, and the trundle bed made somewhat like them was rolled under them during the day and pulled out for service at night. Since they were very low they were used for children's beds, because the child would not hurt himself if he rolled off.

Sometimes these bedsteads were draped from their rails to floor with "frills" made of cloth, the thread of which had been spun, dyed and woven in the home. This drapery was either white or bright-colored and was kept fresh and starched.

Author's wife, Sharon, inside cabin showing 'corded' bedsteads with dowels (Note ceiling logs with flooring above)

The bureau's of this period did not have mirrors, but were more like a chest of drawers of to-day with a small drawer running almost the length and breadth of the top. There were presses which had a small drawer on either side of the top, and the lower section had doors behind which were arranged shelves. The chests of that period resemble somewhat the cedar chests of the present time, but the interior was divided into compartments. The room usually contained a small square top table. The chairs were made with straight backs, and a general mark of the period is the rather sharp top knob arrangement which is carved on the frames which hold the slats for the back.

The dining table was, many times, homemade. Some of them, however were bought. Many of them were dropleaf. A bench for seats were frequently arranged along one side of the dining table next to the wall. There was usually some kind of cupboard in which the dishes were kept. It may have been made of riven boards or plank. Many of them were very much like the safe and cabinet of the present day. There were dishes of ironstone china, pewter, and tin. Biscuit dough was kneaded in wooden bowls call trays. The cakes were made by hand. There were no boards on which to roll it. Pastry for pies was rolled on a cloth, and sometimes a clapboard was planed very smoothly and used in making Johnny cakes. Gourds of different sizes and shapes were used as containers for salt, soap, lard, sugar, coffee and many articles of like kind...also...for dippers.

The cooking utensils consisted of a tin coffee pot, cast iron kettles, ovens, skillets, bakers, and frying pans. The kettles, ovens, skillets, had iron lids, and the frying pans had long handles. All cooking was done on the fire-place, hence the kitchen had chimneys, but if there were no extra room, the living room was also dining room and kitchen. A good stout shovel made by the blacksmith was a...necessary article around these fire-places.

These homes were lighted by tallow candles and grease

lamps. The tallow was made from beef fat and poured into moulds which made the candles. The tallow candle was placed on a stand for use. The grease lamp was sometimes made of iron with a handle and a groove in which the lighted the end of the wick lay. The wick was made of twisted homespun thread and placed in the bowl of the lamp with an end laying in the groove. Lard was poured in the bowl over the wick which was pulled up as it burned away. A candle mould and stand and a grease lamp were essential articles in the home. There were no matches, hence it was necessary to always keep a fire.[121] *Water buckets with gourd dippers were placed on shelves in the kitchen and they were frequently arranged also on the outside wall near the door.*

The implements for work constituted a great part of furniture for these homes. Quilting frames which comprised four pieces of about two inches by two inches by nine feet long were a household necessity, and since all cloth was made in the home, the entire weaving equipment was one of the most important features and house furnishings. Many different articles were used in this cloth making process. Both wool and cotton were used. The material was first spun into thread on the spinning wheel. This thread was wound into hanks on the reel, after which it was perhaps dyed, then quilled on a winding blade and placed in a shuttle for weaving. The thread for the warp was usually bought at this period, but it had to be warped on the warping board, linked, beamed, harnessed, and put into the sley for weaving.

There was always an ash-hopper near the kitchen. The ashes from the fireplace were put in this container and sometimes during the year, usually in the spring, water was poured all over them and lye obtained from the leaching process which was used in making soap. The lye was mixed with hog fat in required proportions and boiled until the

[121] Fraley, Mrs. M. F., Personal Interview, 1934, footnoted by Durbin.

mixture formed balls when dropped in cold water, at which time the soap was considered made.

Details of an ash-hopper have been covered earlier. However, Miss Durbin's description here serves to verify the process, of which generations knew, from the old cabin's days.

The farming implements of the period were the bar-share plow, the diamond eight plow, and the number thirteen plow, the hoe, rake, reap hook, flails, sieve, and cradle. These were made of cast iron and could be found around the house when not in use on the farm.

...many homesteads had to have a well...The water was usually drawn by a windless. The well buckets were made of woods and were rather heavy.

Farmer, grain "cradling" with a five-finger cradle/scythe[122]

As we read the above descriptions of a cabin premises, both inside and out, one can again visualize how either the Wickers originally, or the George's later, lived within and about the old cabin as a rural farm dwelling. Its occupants are shown as "farmers" from the 1850 through the 1870 censuses,

[122] "Department of Conservation Photograph Collection, 1937-1976," *Tennessee Virtual Archive (TeVA).*

thus their living areas would be as described. Even after John Wicker owned the land it was on in 1885, he was shown as a farmer in the 1880 census and again in the 1900 one, even if only there as a park tenant at that time. Dora Patrick Cody's father (later cabin occupant in 1905) was a farmer in that 1900 census.

Proposed Reconstruction of the "War Cabin."

The restoration of the war cabin is an educational feature, and, since the exact construction and furnishings of the house in 1862 are not known, it is proposed that it be reconstructed upon the basis of the information set forth in this paper.

This author certainly agrees with the idea of the old cabin being used as an "educational feature" and it has been over the years and is now being used in "living history" demonstrations at the park. This occurs during battle anniversary celebrations with reenactments and the cabin being used to present a "Women in the War" testimony. At other times the park will bring school tours to the cabin to make a presentation. As stated, it contains two old "corded" bedsteads allowing explanation of the term, "Sleep tight."

Continuing now with the 1934 research papers proposed cabin reconstruction…

The tongue-and-groove floor should be replaced by either rough plank or puncheon (preferably puncheon) which is made of hewed or split logs, planed until they are smooth.

The walls should be ceiled by placing five are six foot riven boards over the cracks between the logs. If these boards were hand planed they would represent the period. The sawed joists should be replaced with either round or hewed logs, and the roof should be entirely covered with riven boards which are two or three feet long.

The chimney can be finished in its present plan of reconstruction. Since rock is common in this section it is suggested that the fireplace can be lined with this material. Let the hearth be built from the ground to the floor level with this sandstone rock. The jambs [?] may be arranged above the fireplace with an insert which would form a shelf on either side. The first log of the house above the fireplace may support the arch or an iron bar can do this. An extra bar should be placed back of the arch support from which the kettles for cooking can be suspended, or the support can be arranged with a crane that will serve this purpose. The fire-place should be framed with a mantel which consists of a plank over the joints on either side and one above the arch over which a shelf is arranged by means of small braces placed under the ends of the plank for support. Place a small hole somewhere in a side of the arch for the handle of the grease lamp.

The amount of furniture in the room could comprise a corded bedstead, bureau, two straight chairs, dining table, cupboard, dishes, cooking utensils, candle mould and stand, grease lamp, and other minor yet significant articles. The complete weaving equipment should be appropriate if space can be found for it.

The farming implements of the time could be placed somewhere about the house, and an ash-hopper nearby would make a very complete setting for the period before the war. A rail or poling fence (unpointed) enclosing the yard would be a characteristic feature.[123]

[Written in script across the blank remainder of this page is "April 1934"]

---

[123] Lear Durbin, "The 'War Cabin'– Its History and Proposed Construction."

Apparently, the furnishings and the farm implements were never made part of the old cabin. Now, at reenactment times and use, various era items are on site but are removed after the event. Because of the remote location of the cabin, any items left unattached year round would probably find their way home with new owners. As mentioned previously the cabin is now locked whereas in early visit days it was open to enter. Even at that, names and initials have still been carved by some, outdoors.

We do not know if the National Park Service fully followed the research writers recommended "Proposed Reconstruction of the 'War Cabin'" in 1934. However, it was probably read and used as a guideline for some parts of reconstruction, at the very least. Some of the features indicated then are evident even today, after two later preservations.

Chapter 13: The 1895 Cabin Condition - Reconstruction Attempts

As stated earlier, in a War Department photo, taken about 1895, if today's cabin, it was in unlivable condition at that time. The photograph itself, which must be accepted as to what the park advises as being the condition of the cabin in that era, is still questionable to this author on several issues. Now the following thoughts are just an opinion, but human error is always possible, for anyone, including this author.

Same picture as earlier, but closer, of the 'War Cabin' in 1895. Courtesy SNMP.

The first thought was that John W. Wicker lived in it at least after he purchased it in 1885. The 1895 picture seems to defy that and thus deems it necessary for John to be living in another cabin on the sixty-five acres that were his until 1896. Questions raised from the picture include that there is no window by the fireplace. Later pictures in 1934 show it there, plus, the trees are different and one missing totally with another seemingly in a different place. The cabin appears square rather than rectangular in shape. Then there's the issue of the 1909 cyclone, or tornado that hit the park and destroyed many of the records there, according to Tim Smith's book. If so, did this 1895 picture survive?

Also, the 1934 paper stated, "With the exception of a few logs which have replaced old ones because of decay, all of the logs in this house are the battle scarred ones of the Louis [sic-'Lewis'] Wicker home." In looking at the 1895 picture, and especially after using a computer zoom, it is difficult to believe many of those logs were salvageable.

Another issue is the number, '#22,' in the corner of the photo. Is this part of the 1934 research papers leaflet mentioned that contained pictures, and merely showing old cabins in the area? Or is it a number from a printed guide made in 1927 by Superintendent Delong Rice first showing tour stops at the park, of which there were twenty-seven? "He placed stakes at each stop with numbers corresponding to a printed handout."[124]

The "Battlefield Guide" issued by the War Department in 1927 was used at Shiloh for several years after administration of the area was assumed by the National Park Service. This publication was supplemented and finally replaced by a five-page mimeographed interpretive guide in 1934, and by a printed information sheet in December, 1937. It was not until 1940, however, that an official two-fold folder,

---

[124] Smith, *This Great Battlefield Shiloh*, 124; *The Untold Story of Shiloh*, 166.

with tour map, was available in the area. The free folder was supplemented by a 16-page illustrated booklet printed in 1941. This sales item was replaced in 1951 by the Shiloh Historical Handbook written by Park Historian Albert Dillahunty.[125]

Of course, the number (#22) probably simply represents a "glass plate negative number" (per Chief Ranger Stacy Allen), taken by the War Department in documenting what was afield in the future park, not only to preserve but to buy with the lands needed.

Later 1934 photos and the research paper indicate an attempt to reconstruct the old cabin after the War Department bought the land it was on in 1897. Implied is an attempt in the 1930's also, plus, the park had it redone by April of 1962 before the 100th battle anniversary. Then the latest rebuilding, restoration and preservation was in 2003, to put it back to battle era days. It was moved slightly and the porch, added in the 1962 effort, was removed but the added window was left in place, presumably to allow light for living history demonstrations done within by the park today, or, simply to ease preservation without reconstructing that wall.

Following is a story from an actual park cabin visitor in the pre-1962 rehab days. This author connected with a Wicker whose father was born in the park area in 1922. This cousin from California e-mailed that she had last visited the park in 1959 with her father, and upon visiting the old cabin there he had told her it "belonged to some relative of his" in the George family.[126] Although not making a definitive connection, his mother had died when he was four in 1926.

However, she was found, before marriage, with her parents in the 1910 McNairy County, Tennessee census (McNairy is just west of Hardin). She is Nancy Lucinda "Lou"

---

[125] Charles E. Shedd, Jr., Park Historian, "A History of Shiloh National Military Park Tennessee."

[126] Linda Wicker, e-mail to the author, April 14, 2007.

George. There are several George families from this county, with an excellent possibility to be kin to William Mansfield George. This cousin has two family connections to the old cabin…her grandfather's surname "Wicker" and her grandmother's maiden name "George." The cabin connections and experiences continue.

Pre-1962, unknown park visitors. Courtesy of SNMP.

One of the 1962 cabin rehab participants preparing for the 100th Anniversary was Wallace Fullwood, Dr. Fullwood's father. In those days he worked as a maintenance man at the park. He indicated that those involved in this effort added the front porch and the wood for it came from a place known as "lover's lane bottom" in the park. An early picture attributed to be Manse George peering from the front door, does not show the porch. However, that photo is questionable to be the cabin, not only by today's rangers, but it clearly has a brick chimney and it appears the George cabin only had the dirt and stick variety. Now there may have been a porch attached before Mr. George bought it on Perry Field and moved it to its present park location. Other park pictures from the 1930's don't show a porch either. However, those from 1962, on, do show it attached.

Apparently the cabin was moved slightly (thirteen degrees according to Ranger Tom Parson) in 1962. Pictures show it was stripped of roof, ceiling and chinking, braced and then rehabbed. The stick and dirt chimney was replaced with a new one. Mr. Fullwood indicated they used earth containing clay and added some cement to it.

One of the celebrants attending the 1962 anniversary was Dora Patrick Cody, who again, is Dr. Ronnie Fullwood's grandmother. A picture was taken of her standing under the old cabin's window where she had told of her father falling out the opening during a sleepwalking episode in 1905. A newspaper story has also been written about her history.

1962 rehab of the cabin. Courtesy of SNMP.

1962, Dora (Patrick) Cody at the cabin window.
Courtesy of Dr. Ronnie Fullwood

Post-1962 picture of unknown visitors. Courtesy of SNMP.

Over the next forty years, visitors to the park would continue to stop at what is shown as the "W. Manse George Cabin." It would be open to go inside to look, although access to the area above the ceiling via the wooden steps was denied by padlocked bars.

One could still step up to see within this supposed original sleeping area in what might be called an attic or full loft. On the main floor itself, this author, at over six feet tall, could not stand up fully within or even enter the doors without ducking down even further.

Time would eventually begin to erode the chimney and other aspects of the cabin. Thus, another rehab was in order (2003) and afterwards the cabin was locked as it remains today. However, it may be possible to see inside if one can arrange ahead of time for a ranger to unlock it.

So in 2003, the latest restoration, rehabilitation and preservation of the old cabin were conducted by the park personnel, headed by Ranger Tom Parson. In an irony, shared by him personally, are pictures from 1980 at the cabin, whereby he was a visitor to the park. At that time he didn't know he would return one day as a park ranger to become the leader of the 2003 cabin facelift.

Cabin visitor Tom Parson in 1980. Courtesy of Tom.

Tom's park crew removed the porch in reestablishing battle-era days and restored the crumbling chimney. His specific scope from his project report included the following:

Removing the porch
Straightening the bulging north wall
Repositioning the cabin
Replacing the roof
Chinking and daubing the walls
Rebuilding the chimney[127]

Although fully unknown because of so many rehab efforts since the late 1890's, bullet holes, as stated, may still be evident in the cabin today, a reminder of its history and survival. One truly wonders, though, if any original 'Wicker-used' wood still remains?

2003 photo by Ranger Tom Parson, heading up the rehab.

[127] Thomas E. Parson, "Manse George Cabin, Preservation Project, Phase I, 2003," SNMP.

Tom and his crew would move the cabin back to its original position. "Through the use of historic base maps Chief Ranger/Historian Stacy Allen determined that the cabin should be turned 13 degrees to the south-east to conform to its traditional facing."[128]

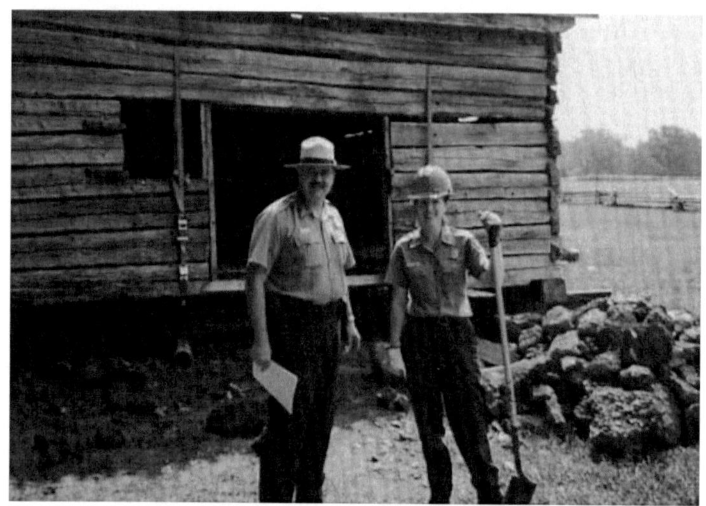

Chief Ranger Allen (left) with Ranger Ashley Ball. Courtesy of SNMP.

The cabin was relocated to this site in 1862 after the battle, not before. Therefore, one supposes if known where it stood, being restored to a 'battle days' location might necessitate a move back to Perry Field at the park entrance. However, where it stands is not as important as the fact that it stands. As indicated before, though, current NPS standards were followed for such.

For those interested, one can see the NPS preservation brief 26 online at:

http://www.cr.nps.gov/hps/tps/briefs/brief26.htm#Traditional%20Log%20Construction

---

[128] Ibid.

2003 park work crew. Courtesy of SNMP.

Chapter 14: "Here Comes Hollywood" And More Recent Events, Photos

Even the old cabin has become "Hollywood" famous. In the fall of 1990, Ken Burns included a shot of it in his documentary film, *The Civil War*. Just before it appeared on the screen in the documentary, film consultant and well-known Civil War author Shelby Foote had said: "Shiloh had the same number of casualties as Waterloo." Narrator David McCullough then reported the following as the old cabin came on the screen, "Years afterward a Union veteran said, 'The most a soldier could say of any fight was, I was worse scared than I was at Shiloh.'" In the next camera view from the Peach Orchard (where you can hear birds in the background, singing in the pink-blossomed trees), the narrator continued by saying, "Shiloh is a Hebrew word, meaning 'Place of Peace.'"

Author's captured photo from tape of Ken Burns "The Civil War" airing on PBS station KERA in Denton, Texas, 2002.

The park has had, and the old cabin witnessed, some field archeology by the University of Memphis, first in 1999 and then again in 2000, attempting to determine information about private historic buildings or the farmers who built them. The first online abstract below is by Dr. Ellen Shlasko and grad-student Claire Henline; the 2nd by Dr. Shlasko:

A HOUSE OF SOME PRETENSION: HISTORICAL ARCHAEOLOGY AT SHILOH NATIONAL MILITARY PARK, 1999. In the spring of 1999, the University of Memphis, Department of Anthropology ran an archaeological field school at the Shiloh National Military Park. The students located and excavated an antebellum farmstead, one of approximately 70 structures that stood in the area at the time of the battle. Although the Shiloh area was, at the time, home to a number of farm families, little physical evidence of their lives remains on the park. This excavation was the first step in a larger project that will increase our knowledge of these yeoman farmers and the area in which they lived.

WHERE WAS WIDOW BELL'S BARN? CONTINUING RESEARCH AT SHILOH NATIONAL MILITARY PARK. This paper presents the results of archaeological testing at Shiloh National Military Park, conducted by the University of Memphis. The goal of the survey was to locate historic buildings in a field adjacent to the Peach Orchard, the scene of heavy fighting during the battle of Shiloh. Historic maps place two structures in this area, but the exact location, age, form and function of the buildings are unknown. In order to recover this information, the researchers used both metal detector survey and shovel testing, with varying results.[129]

---

[129] Tennessee Archeology Net, hosted by Dr. Kevin E. Smith, Department of Sociology and Anthropology, Middle Tennessee State University, "Current Research in Tennessee Archaeology Annual Meeting Abstracts – 1994-2007," http://frank.mtsu.edu/~kesmith/TNARCH/CRITA/CRITA_Abstracts.html.

(See Appendix #4 for excavation results)

The initial "farmstead" was up the road (north) from the old cabin, per Chief Ranger Stacy Allen. The latter study would have been in the old cabin's front yard practically, as it is of course on Sarah Bell's old land next to the peach orchard and her old cotton field.

Also in about this era, the park confirmed through ground penetrating radar (GPR), the existence of a Tilghman/Tillman family cemetery in the forested area behind now Perry Field or near the old Tilghman residence. This is on some of the same lands Wicker and then Perry owned pre-battle, where the old cabin use to stand. Tilghman owned it later. In the middle of Perry Field, one can see remnants from one of these family homes as either an old well and/or foundation stones. Could they be from the old cabins days there?

Possible foundation or well remains (foreground) of Tilghman home, mentioned above, on today's Perry Field. Maybe even from the old cabin's days there? Author's photo.

On April 7, 2001, a "companion" log structure to the old cabin was dedicated at Shiloh. That would be the Shiloh Church replica. It was a project of the local Sons of Confederate Veterans Camp at Shiloh. However, soon others such as the United Daughters of the Confederacy, the Sons of Union Veterans, and, Shiloh National Military Park itself joined in the rebuilding effort.[130] Now there are two old historic log buildings in the park, and, whether one is not original and one only partially, their historic value remains valid.

Inside of replicated Shiloh Church. Author's photo in 2005.

In 2002, this author attended the 140th Anniversary battle celebration. It was another personal chance to visit the old cabin and provided others the same opportunity. Especially interesting was the 'Women in the War' living history demonstration to be conducted at the old cabin. There, pictures were taken and one could see Confederate women re-enactors

[130] Fullwood, *Shiloh's House of Peace*, 81-82.

attired in long dresses and bonnets with spinning wheel and butter churn. Ironically, they were from a re-enactment group near this author's home in Texas.

There was also a medical demonstration nearby and one wondered if the old cabin had been used as a field hospital at any time, even before any rightful residents were allowed back in Shiloh? If so, interestingly, it was learned medical staff in the field during the Civil War wore green and yellow on their uniforms to identify themselves, and, Clara Barton's Red Cross was not used until post-war.

The 'Women in the War' demonstration, or the like at the old cabin, apparently had been going on for some time, as reported by Miss Lear Durbin in the draft notes from her research paper in 1934. In them she stated, "...members of the Park's Women's Organization will be demonstrating living conditions of the Manse George family." Since the battle anniversary would be coming up in early April, 1934, the assumption is that the demonstration, of which she wrote in the future tense, would be occurring then.

'Women in the War' at the 2002 battle anniversary. Author's photo.

Author's note: On February 17, 1958, Miss Lear Pearl Durbin passed away and was buried in Shiloh Church Cemetery. Lear was born at Shiloh on April Fools Day, 1884. By at least 1910, as reported, she was a local teacher there. Probably sometime between 1922 and 1930, based on the name of the college, she received a Bachelor of Arts from West Kentucky State Teachers College. Then in August, 1930 a Masters of Art in History at George Peabody College for Teachers, now part of Vanderbilt. Owed her is a great debt, this CWA writer, for her no-longer-latent cabin data in this work. One of 192 women selected nationwide in 1934 for this program, as stated. Thank you Miss Durbin.

Gravestone of local teacher, Lear Durbin, Shiloh Cemetery. Said of her: "A great teacher." "A very smart woman." Author's 2007 photo.

In a June, 2005 visit, the Tennessee monument dedication was attended where Park Superintendent Woody Harrell gave the welcome. Pictures were taken of the latest rehab of the cabin, as well as at the dedication ceremony. Once again, it brought cabin visitors.

Welcoming address, Park Superintendent Woody Harrell

The State of Tennessee had never erected a monument at the park. Individual ones for state military units were there but none for the state itself. It is a beautiful monument, entitled "Passing of Honor," designed by a Texan not far from this author's home and depicting a fallen Confederate Flag Bearer with one comrade coming to his aide and another standing sentinel with rifle in hand.

This author harkened back to a family story of a 2nd great grandfather, Roderick Gaines Wicker (who helped build and initially lived in the old cabin), falling at Shiloh, reported earlier in this work as being a flag bearer. It has come to this author's attention that, as an artilleryman, Roderick more than likely was a forward flagman for an artillery battery. Their job was to take a flag on a pole and move to another desired position and wave the flag to signal where to move to next. The Union would have tried to shoot him in order to prevent the move. Nonetheless, cold chills were in order as a response to the above-mentioned unveiled statue.

New Tennessee Monument, June 2005. Author's photo.

Dedication day 2005; re-enactors of both war sides. Author's photo. (Ranger/Author Tim Smith, 4th Union soldier to the right of the flag.)

Today it's 2008, and one can find several cabin photos and references online, a long way for the old cabin to come, from little technology when it was built by 1849, to today's cyberspace world. Hopefully this author has done it justice.

Online photos:

Unfinished chimney 2003-2004 Alan Zirkle photo (used by permission)

SNMP photo of living history demonstration

Jackson Sun photo

CivilWarAlbum.com photo

Chapter 15: A Recap, And Other Cabin/Park Experiences

What the old cabin has seen; produce and people going to the Tennessee River, a newly wedded couple in August of 1849, a census taker in 1850 from Savannah, a new owner by 1853, then another by 1855 to have a field so named after, a new census taker from Hamburg to the south in 1860, then the sights and sounds of bloody battle, to be cover for sharpshooters, to survive, only to be then disassembled and moved, ironically next door to it's original family. Then it was left vacant sometime after 1870 or later and a state of ruin set in, a picture was taken by 1895, its land sold to the USA in 1897 for a park to preserve it. Touches of reconstruction, first to allow tenants, then again in 1934 and a research paper written about it. Then again it had a facelift in 1962 to celebrate 100 years since the great battle there. Finally, it's most recent 2003 rehab by the park. Over the years it saw…a dusting of snow (even 18 inches once), a rainbow,

SNMP online; pre-2003 photo by Ranger Josh Clemons.

the smoke of cannon, soldiers coming home, the shooting of a neighbor, the winds of a cyclone, veterans returning to remember, statues and monuments set about it, postal deliveries from Savannah, then Hamburg, fires from homes or forest, rains that pelted down, an ice storm, archeologists digging in the field beyond. Visitors aplenty, of all ages, from all places, even foreign, have passed through it's doors, at least until time and human behavior have forced it to be under lock and key, as it is today. It has weathered its world yet gives no ground; standing for what it does…a relic of the past.

In the early park years, what brought people to Shiloh where they could end up seeing the old cabin while there (if not occupied and maybe even then) and how did they come? The following reports are given:

The only major change in this period was the increase of steamboat traffic on the Tennessee, with its consequent benefits to the inhabitants of the region. The principal steamboat line at this period was the Evansville and Tennessee River Packet Company, the line which for many years brought visitors to Shiloh Park.[131]

One of the most productive ways of raising money in the early 1900's at Shiloh was to tap the constant flow of veterans and visitors who came to the battlefield by way of steamboats. Many…would drive tourists around by horse and wagon and would often reap generous donations from the folks up north. The 30th of May was one of the most popular times for visitors at Shiloh. On many occasions local farmers would be plowing corn in the nearby river bottom and when they heard the steamboat blow its whistle at Pittsburg Landing they would unhitch from the plow immediately and hitch to their wagons and buggies knowing they could make more money

---

[131] Lera Durbin, "Five Years of War" in ms. History of Hardin County, Shiloh NMP, 1934, p. 2., quoted online by Charles E. Shedd, Jr., Park Historian, "A History of Shiloh National Military Park Tennessee."

guiding the tourists over the park. [132]

Those visitors came primarily to see dedications of state monuments and for other important celebrations. This provided opportunities to visit the old cabin, as shown by the details in the following NPS online history from 1954 by Charles Shedd:

Dedications of State Monuments

On June 6, 1902, the first monument dedication took place on the field of Shiloh when 2,000 persons assembled for the transfer of 34 Ohio regimental monuments to the Federal Government. Presentation of the monuments was made by Judge David F. Pugh of Ohio, and acceptance on behalf of the Federal Government was made by Commission Chairman Cadle.

In reference to the above, in the previously mentioned diary started January 1, 1901 and kept by Sarah Armintha Wicker, through to her 21st birthday on June 16, 1902, she reports the following. It is just ten days before she ceased keeping her diary:

June 6, 1902. Friday Lee went to the bottom and plowed. Enos, Frank, Lucy McDaniel and I went to Pitsburgh [sic]. The Ohio folks dedicated their monuments.

As the first monument dedication at the park, it was obviously news shared with, and, important to the locals as well. Now back to Mr. Shedd's reporting:

The next state dedication took place on April 6 and 7, 1903, the 41st anniversary of the battle, when five river

[132] Fullwood, *Shiloh's House of Peace*, 67.

steamers brought hundreds of Indiana veterans and their families to the park, where they were met by additional hundreds of southerners, gathered to witness the dedication of 21 monuments to Indiana units which participated in the battle.

The monuments were presented to the Government by Indiana Governor Winfield T. Durbin, and accepted by William Cary Sanger, Assistant Secretary of War. The principal address of the meeting was given by the famous Senator Albert J. Beveridge of Indiana. A feature of the program was the recitation of the poem "The Name of Old Glory" by its author James Witcomb Riley.

The following fall, on November 12, 1903, a monument was dedicated to the only eastern regiment to fight in the Battle of Shiloh - the 77th Pennsylvania. A party of 100 citizens of the Keystone State including Governor Samuel W. Pennypacker, arrived on the steamer Clyde to present the monument in Review Field, where it was accepted on behalf of the Secretary of War by Commission Chairman Cadle.

On May 17-18, 1904, the State of Illinois dedicated 40 monuments to her troops on the battlefield of Shiloh. One of these monuments was the Illinois State Memorial, one of the most imposing on the field. Colonel Cadle accepted the monuments on behalf of the Federal Government, and an address was made by the venerable Confederate General Basil Duke. General Duke expressed the meaning of the battlefield preservation when he said:

"When a people renders such honors to the heroic dead it honors itself. The national care bestowed on this historic spot is as much a potent lesson to the future as a sacred duty to the past, for it commemorates the virtues without which nations can not survive. May those who fell here never be forgotten, and may these monuments erected to their memory remain as enduring admonitions to the youth of succeeding generations, to love and serve their country equally as well."

On August 22, 1905, Tennessee became the first former

Confederate State to be represented by a memorial on the field when veterans of the regiemnt [sic] dedicated a monument to the 2nd Tennessee Infantry. Three thousand persons from Tennessee and neighboring states assembled to watch the unveiling and hear the remarks of General Duke, who accepted the monument on behalf of the United States. [Remember, the Patrick's were living in the old cabin in 1905]

On the 44th anniversary of the battle, April 7, 1906, Governor James O. Davidson and party from Wisconsin presented that State's memorial to the Park Commission. Chairman Cadle accepted for the Commission, and remarks were made by Governor Davidson and General Duke.

After a prolonged disagreement about text on two of its regimental monuments, the State of Iowa, on November 23, 1906, dedicated 11 unit markers and the Iowa State Monument. Presentation was made by Iowa's Governor Albert B. Cummins, and the memorials were accepted for the park by Commissioner Cadle. This dedication at Shiloh was the last in a series made by the Iowa delegation. Dedications of Iowa monuments during the previous week had been made at Vicksburg, Andersonville, Georgia, and Chattanooga.

On May 7, 1907, another former Confederate State dedicated a memorial to its Shiloh troops, when a small delegation from Alabama braved a heavy rain to present the State Monument to the Commission. The Alabama Monument was erected with donations from the State's chapters of the United Daughters of the Confederacy. Chairman Cadle accepted the memorial on behalf of the Federal Government.

Almost a year later, on April 10, 1908, the next state dedication occurred when Governor John A. Johnson and a delegation from Minnesota presented a memorial to that State's single unit which participated in the battle. The monument, to the First Battery, Minnesota Light Artillery, was accepted by Commissioner Cadle, and addresses were made by Governor Johnson and General Duke.

A memorial "to the brave Confederate dead of Arkansas who fell on this battlefield" was dedicated by that State's U.D.C. chapters on September 6, 1911. The dedication address was made by General R.G. Shaver, commander of the brigade at Shiloh which contained many Arkansas troops. The monument was accepted on behalf of the Commission by Chairman Reed.

With the passage of years, dedications of battlefield memorials became less frequent. It was not until 1915 that another state was represented on the field, when Dr. Y.R. Lemonnier, a former private of the regiment, dedicated a monument to the famous Crescent Louisiana Regiment of New Orleans on Memorial Day.

On May 17, 1917, the largest dedication ceremony in Shiloh's history occurred when the National United Daughters of the Confederacy unveiled the striking Confederate Memorial before a crowd of 15,000 persons.

No doubt the above ceremony, with its large crowd, brought another banner day of visitors to the old cabin. Its family occupants over the years were apparently of a mostly Confederate persuasion, as many of those would have necessarily been this day.

The U.D.C. Director of the Shiloh Monument Committee reported that visitors came "on boats, on horseback, in carriages and in automobiles from distant points in Alabama, Mississippi, Kentucky and Tennessee." Congressman E.S. Candler, Jr., of Mississippi, was master of ceremonies, and the welcoming address was made by Governor Tom Rye of Tennessee. Mrs. Cordelia Powell Odenheimer presented the monument to the Federal Government, represented on this occasion by Park Superintendent DeLong Rice. Frederick Hibbard, sculptor of the memorial, was present. The principal address was made by the Rt. Rev. Thomas F. Gailor, Bishop of Tennessee, and following this talk a letter from President Woodrow Wilson was read.

The last state monument to be dedicated on the field was to the troops from Michigan who engaged in the battle. On Memorial Day, 1919, a delegation headed by Michigan Governor Albert E. Sleeper, and including Senator Roy M. Watkins, Representative Charles A. Weissert, and other dignitaries of the State, took part in the presentation of the monument. Acceptance on behalf of the United States Government was made by Park Director DeLong Rice.

Other Important Celebrations

During the early years of the park's existence, most programs of outstanding interest were those held in conjunction with the memorial dedications described above. There were, however, some celebrations of more than routine interest in the area.

Veterans organizations, in particular the Association of Battle of Shiloh Survivors, held their annual reunions on the battlefield for many years. On April 6-7, 1907, the Survivors Association held its first reunion on the battlefield, in a joint meeting with hundreds of former Confederates. This reunion, as was true with many, did not feature a formal program, but was devoted to touring the battlefield, and reminiscing with "old soldiers", gray and blue alike, who had heard the guns of Shiloh.

Due to difficult travel conditions prior to 1914, attendance at park celebrations usually was not large. The largest crowd to attend a celebration at the park during the first 15 years of its existence was present on Memorial Day, 1906, when a gathering estimated to number as many as 12,000 persons thronged the park, to decorate graves and participate in the patriotic program. A member of the park staff, reporting the large attendance, commented, "The woods were full."

For many years a Memorial Day weather "jinx" marred the annual celebration with remarkable regularity. A typical report for the day noted that "The 30th of May brought the customary rain, early in the morning, so the crowd was very small."

On April 6 and 7, 1912, the 50th anniversary of the battle, 300 members of the Hornets' Nest Brigade, a veterans organization made up of Federal troops who had fought in the Hornets' Nest, held a memorial program at the park. The Iowa Monument, repaired following its damage in the cyclone of 1909, was rededicated, Governor B.F. Carroll of Iowa making the principal address.

In 1920, the first of the famous "Shiloh Sings" took place. This program, held each year early in September, still attracts the largest crowds of the year to the park, to hear vocal groups from throughout the South present a program usually lasting four to six hours. [Apparently these are no longer held]

On April 6 and 7, 1935, not quite two years after Shiloh became part of the National Park Service, park personnel carried out a program of widespread interest commemorating the 73rd anniversary of the battle. A special cachet to be stamped on mail originating at the park was designed by Historical Assistant Randle B. Truett. On April 6 the cachet was stamped in red, memorializing the Confederate Army, while on the 7th the stamp was in blue, in memory of the Union forces. One thousand six hundred and fifty seven requests for envelopes bearing the special stamp were received from collectors throughout the world. In addition to this feature, two radio addresses on the subject "Shiloh-1862 and 1935" were given; one from Nashville, Tennessee, by Historical Assistant George F. Emery, Stones River National Military Park, and the other from Memphis, by Historical Assistant W.W. Luckett of

Shiloh.

A program at the park, August 10, 1941, celebrated the 25th anniversary of the National Park Service. Congressman Ross Collins of Mississippi delivered the principal address, calling for American preparedness for a war then only a few months away. The speech was dramatically underscored by the presence of 7,000 troops of the 33rd Division pouring into the park, to bivouac for the night enroute to the memorable Louisiana maneuvers of 1941.

Here is inserted an excerpt about a park visitor, and therefore potential cabin visitor, during another battle anniversary celebration, this one in 1947. On April 6 and 7 of that year one Shelby Foote, a now deceased author but today still well-known as a Civil War historian, "slept on the battlefield and made a charge with a stick bayonet," before returning home to begin the novel, *Shiloh.*[133] Now back to Shedd's history:

For the celebration of the 90th anniversary of the Battle of Shiloh, on April 6, 1952, the Tennessee Historical Society and the West Tennessee Historical Society jointly sponsored a program at the park. Guests included novelists William Faulkner, Claude Gentry, and Shelby Foote; southern historians Stanley Horn and Dr. Marshall Wingfield, and Mrs. Maggie J. Hardin, reputed to be the only surviving widow of a Shiloh veteran. Superintendent Ira B. Lykes welcomed the crowd of more than 2,500 persons assembled in the historic Peach Orchard, and Dr. Otto Eisenschimi, author of several popular historical works, made the principal address on the battle.

Worthy to note here is that the above celebration staged at the Peach Orchard undoubtedly at least brought within sight,

[133] C. Stuart Chapman, *Shelby Foote, A Writer's Life* (Jackson: University of Mississippi Press, 2003), 106.

the largest concentration of visitors next to the old cabin, if not in it to visit individually as well. Again, back to Shedd's history:

Probably the largest anniversary celebration in the park's history occurred on April 4, 1954, commemorating the 92nd anniversary of the battle. Of particular interest was the presence of Major General U.S. Grant, 3rd, grandson of the commander of the Federal Army of the Tennessee at Shiloh, and Colonel William B. Ruggles, grandson of Brigadier General Daniel Ruggles, Confederate divisional commander in the battle. Principal speakers for the occasion were Senator Estes Kefauver of Tennessee, and Dr. Kenneth P. Williams, professor of mathematics at Indiana University and a top-ranking student of Civil War military history. Master of Ceremonies for the program was Mr. Hillory B. Tolson, assistant director of the National Park Service. A crowd estimated at more than 10,000 persons was present in the park during the program.

The above celebration, as the largest yet by 1954, undoubtedly brought many cabin visitors, also. Then Mr. Shedd reports on an ice storm in 1951. Details from Shedd:

The Ice Storm of January, 1951

Nature, for the most part, has been kind to Shiloh and no subsequent natural disasters have equalled [sic] the cyclone of 1909 in destruction of park values. However, in late January 1951, an ice storm gripped the area, leaving in its wake the destruction of hundreds of trees and the mutilation of thousands more.

Fortunately no serious structural damage was suffered by park buildings, although burst water pipes and failure of electrical power caused considerable hardship. The 17-mile telephone line to Corinth was wiped out, and for several days the park was in a virtual state of isolation.

Today, almost four years [1954] after the storm, evidence of its fury is still visible in the form of shattered, bent and dying trees. While many trees are dying from more immediate causes, their susceptibility to other forms of attack may be traced directly to the destructive effects of the ice storm.[134]

'Survivor' becomes an appropriate name for the cabin at Shiloh. Not only did it survive the battle in 1862, then survive the cyclone in 1909 but also survived this ice storm.

Over the years, just who were the most important visitors at the old cabin? Some idea can be taken from those who made Shiloh National Military Park what it is today, as stated in Timothy B. Smith's book, *This Great Battlefield of Shiloh*. In his preface he offers a "word of thanks that must go to the veterans of Shiloh…who fought here…and returned forty years later to build a park. To men such as Cornelius Cadle, Atwell Thompson, and especially D. W. Reed, thank you for preserving the heritage of Shiloh…"[135]

And part of that heritage preserved has to be the cabin that witnessed much over the years, even more than the battle days and beyond. It was in essence a "teenager" when the battle broke out, having been built some thirteen years before when it housed the Wicker family. However it "came of age" soon, surviving the battle blight. Then it was dismantled, moved, and like a "Phoenix bird rising from the ashes," was taken again to its intended destiny…that of housing a family, the George's. Once again it apparently had to be "re-born" in the late 1890,'s after it had "come full circle" and been bought and sold by a member of the Wicker family, then it was finally

---

[134] Charles E. Shedd, Jr., Park Historian, "A History of Shiloh National Military Park Tennessee."
[135] Smith, *This Great Battlefield of Shiloh*, Preface.

rescued as the "War Cabin."

For any visitor's to the cabin today, located by the parking area beside the Peach Orchard near the cabin, is the park's display board. Their narrative states the following:

At the time of the battle this land was owned and farmed by the W. Manse George family. When the fighting started, the family fled. Later they returned to find their home burned and possessions destroyed. After the battle, a cabin from another part of the battlefield was moved here to replace the one swept away by war. The short path to your right leads to this historic building.

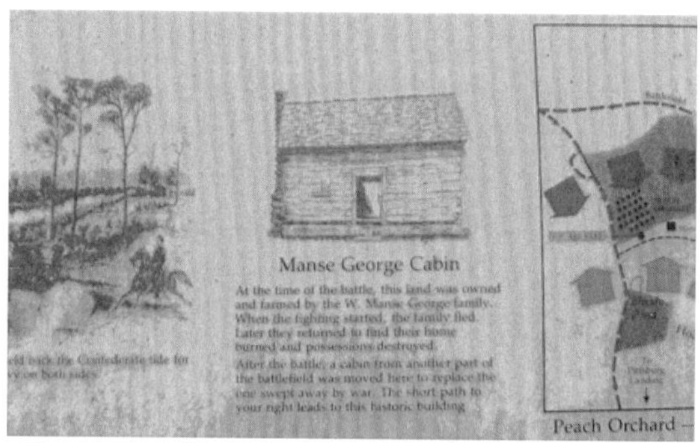

Current park on-site view board. Author's photo.

Closing:
Visit The Cabin With The Author

Although I may have to view the cabin as only "originally" built by my ancestor and that its walls may be only symbolic today, it, together with Shiloh Church, still stand as reminders in the middle of this great battlefield, with military evidence and memorials all around, that common everyday people once lived here. They had their lives totally disrupted by the events of April 6-7, 1862. Homes and crops ruined, personal property left behind, destroyed, and in some cases life was lost, both civilian and soldier of those who called Shiloh home, and the same holds true for any pre-battle occupants of the old cabin; the silent, surviving witness of the military storm and subsequent carnage.

I like to visit the old cabin. When I go there, sometimes other visitors are around. They come, they see, they soon move on, but, I like to tarry a bit. I let my imagination run some and wonder, as I said in my introduction, "If walls could talk…" It is just there, innate, unfeeling, wooden property upon the land. Those walls don't speak, but if you listen carefully, they echo back; the laughter of children, the crying baby, the moaning of pain, the wailing over lost life, Christmas carols chimed in on and also hymns of Gospel. The whisking sound that broom reeds make upon the plank floor, the whirring of a spinning wheel, embers crackling in the fireplace, alit to warm the evening meal of stew bubbling in the kettle suspended over the fire, the aroma of food filling the room.

Talk of the day resounds from the table where the men of the family have gathered after a day's toiling in the fields, or hunting in the bottoms or fishing from the shores of the Tennessee; chores completed, animals fed and put to their bed, hands and faces washed, awaiting the offering of first, a thanks to God, then that which the loving ladies' hands of the family prepared for all. The smoke from the chimney rises out into the evening air and dissipates to the point of a lazy haze that still fills ones nostrils with the smell of spent wood. Through the two doors and out the lone window travel the tales therein…that of life, and death; sleeping, eating, bathing, cooking, weaving, cleaning rifles, preparing fishing lines, praying and Bible reading by tallow candle, firelight and someday coal-oil lamps. Book learning for the children, skinned shins doctored, tales to tuck them in a trundle bed by, curious questions answered, all in a day's life. Some require their bed cords to be wound up, bringing a, "Sleep tight."

A new day brings hog killing, soap making from lye, corn or cotton planted, a squirrel for the stew or a turkey for the table; eggs to gather, cows to milk, trips to a town or to Shiloh Church. Over time, babies are born there, ill or infirm die there. The maladies of the day are no respecter of age or agronomy…fevers and fires, headaches and hailstones.

If walls could talk or see, the tales of life, the history of heritage, the sights and smells of savored sanctity, written upon the windows of time and released through the doors of a dwelling that says so much to us. All one has to do is listen, be still and let your mind take you through the quiet of the moment into the world of the old cabin. It bears its history proudly, its scars mark its destiny, its creation its place in time, this lone survivor at Shiloh. Oh, if only those walls could talk…of the days of Sunday Shiloh remembered...this lone survivor there.

Bits and Pieces of Me

Every place I visit, where my ancestors belie,
There locked into memory, is where I do lie.
I am them and they too are, bits and pieces of me,
Those who lay interred in earth, at a silent cemetery.

I am the one who walked among the highland hills of Scotland,
The one who tilled the rich dark soil in old Bavarialand.
I stood and died on Shiloh's hill in a battle on the Tennessee,
'Twas me who o'er looked a Texas prairie, as far an eye can see.

Farm and toil, travail and task, they are bits and pieces of me,
That lie at rest in shadowed graves, in a lonely cemetery.
There, stones grow old and weather away, fading with each day,
And beneath them are the tales of life that now have slipped away.

They speak no more, they see no more, they lie in silent death,
Although the wind does blow around, in them there is no breath.
I stand upon their hallowed ground, their living testimony,
As I am them and they too are, bits and pieces of me.

Duane Helweg

Update note: Since first publication, one of Lewis and Flora Wicker's sons, who helped build the original cabin and live in it, has been located out-of-state after the 1850 census. Andrew J. Wicker in that census is Andrew Jackson Wicker, so-named after the 7th U. S. president (1829-1837) from Tennessee, left Hardin after 1850 and is in Kentucky by 1858 but remains unfound if in the war. Finding the full name of Andrew helps establish the full name of "Jasper" as shown in this work now as Lewis Jasper Wicker. Since Jasper's father was also given named Lewis, logic would say that likely the younger one may have been called by his middle name to avoid confusion.

Author's note: When I think of my 2nd great grandfather, Roderick Gaines Wicker, apparently lying in a mass Confederate grave at Shiloh, and the history of his father and family building the old cabin that remains there, I'm reminded of a quote from famed Civil War author, Shelby Foote. As stated by C. Stuart Chapman, in the book *Shelby Foote: A Writer's Life*, the great grandfather of Shelby, Henry Foote, had fought at Shiloh and Shelby had visited there many times, of which he said, "For me, something emanates from that ground, the way memory sometimes leaps up at you unexpectedly."

I, too, feel the same…when I'm at Shiloh.

Bibliography

Allen, Stacy D., Historian, Shiloh National Military Park. "Shiloh!." *Blue & Gray, A Visitor's Guide*, 2001.

---. "'*If He Had Less Rank*,' Lewis Wallace." *Grant's Lieutenant's from Cairo to Vicksburg.* Edited by Steven E. Woodworth. Lawrence, KS: University Press of Kansas, 2001.

Betts, Vicki. "A Revelation of War: Civilians in Hardin County, Tennessee, Spring, 1862." http://www.uttyler.edu/vbetts/shiloh.htm.

Bomberger, Bruce D. "The Preservation and Repair of Historic Log Buildings." National Park Service Preservation Brief 26. http://www.nps.gov/history/hps/tps/briefs/brief26.htm.

Brazelton, B. G. *A History of Hardin County, Tennessee.* Nashville, TN: Cumberland Presbyterian Publishing House, 1885, Chapter XIV, at TNGENWEB. Transcribed by Gene Hosey. http://www.geocities.com/Heartland/Meadows/6273/hardin/braz_title.html.

Cain, Rosanne. Transcription. "1850 Census for Hardin County," *Hardin County, Tennessee History & Genealogy.* http://ftp.rootsweb.ancestry.com/pub/usgenweb/tn/hardin/census/1850/ (USGenWeb).

"Captain J. W. Phillips' Tennessee Light Artillery Company, 'Johnston Light Artillery.'" *Tennesseans in the Civil War, Confederate Artillery Units.* www.tngenweb.org/civilwar/csaart/phillips.html.

"Catfish Hotel – History." The Catfish Hotel. http://catfishhotel.com/history.htm.

Chapman, C. Stuart. *Shelby Foote, A Writer's Life.* Jackson: University of Mississippi Press, 2003.

Cotton, Reverend Thomas. "The Cross and the Flag." 1899. Copy of typewritten work courtesy of Larry DeBerry, Shiloh, TN.

Cunningham, O. Edward. *Shiloh and the Western Campaign of 1862.* Edited by Gary D. Joiner and Timothy B. Smith. New York, NY: Savas Beatie LLC, 2007.

Daniel, Larry J. *Shiloh: The Battle that Changed the Civil War.* New York: Touchstone/Simon & Shuster, 1997.

"Department of Conservation Photograph Collection, 1937-1976." *Tennessee Virtual Archive (TeVA).* A program of the Tennessee State Library and Archives. http://tsla-teva.state.tn.us/.

"Diary of Sarah Arminta Wicker Delaney, January 1, 1901-June 16, 1902."

Dictionary and Thesaurus - Merriam-Webster Online. http://www.merriam-webster.com.

Dillahunty, Albert. *Shiloh National Military Park, Tennessee* (1955). National Park Service Historical Handbook Series No. 10, Washington, D. C., Reprinted 1961. www.nps.gov/history/history/online_books/hh/10/index.htm#top.

Downing, Beverly. "I Do!" *Family Chronicle, The Magazine for Families Researching Their Roots.* http://www.familychronicle.com/MarriageCustoms.html.

Durbin, Lear, Assistant Historian, Civil Works Administration, Shiloh National Military Park, TN. "The 'War Cabin'– It's History and Proposed Construction." Research paper, SNMP, April, 1934.

---. Assistant Historian, Civil Works Administration, Shiloh National Military Park, TN. "Stick-and-Dirt Chimney." Research paper, SNMP, 1934.

---. "Economic and Social Development of Hardin County Tennessee Since 1865." Thesis for Master of Arts in History degree, George Peabody College for Teachers, August 1930. Copy courtesy of Connie Lewis, Assistant Director/Reference & Genealogy, Hardin County Public Library.

---. "Five Years of War." In ms. History of Hardin County, Shiloh NMP, 1934, p. 2. Quoted in Charles E. Shedd, Jr., Park Historian, "A History of Shiloh National Military Park Tennessee." http://www.nps.gov/archive/shil/admhisint3.htm.

Family history document by Juanita Martin.

Foote, Shelby. *Shiloh.* 1991 ed. New York: Vintage/Random House, 1952.

Frank, Joseph Allen and George A. Reaves. *"Seeing the Elephant" Raw Recruits at the Battle of Shiloh.* Urbana and Chicago: University of Illinois Press, 2003.

Fullwood, Dr. Ronnie. *Shiloh's House of Peace: The Church That Named the Battle*. Selmer, TN; G & P Printing Services, 2003.

George Washington Carver National Monument, National Park Service. Diamond, MO. "Carver Trail Tour, The Ash Hopper." http://www.nps.gov/archive/gwca/expanded/trail_7.htm.

Grant, U. S. "The Battle of Shiloh." *The Century Magazine*, Vol. XXIX, No. 4, Feb., 1885. http://cdl.library.cornell.edu/cgi-bin/moa/sgml/moa-idx?notisid=ABP2287-0029-136.

---. *Personal Memoirs of U. S. Grant.* 1885. The Project Gutenberg Ebook of Personal Memoirs of U. S. Grant, Complete. June 2004. http://www.gutenberg.org/files/4367/4367-h/4367-h.htm.

Harrell, Edward R. Transcriber. *Savannah Courier.* Newspaper published in Hardin County, Savannah, Tennessee, transcriptions, 1885-1901. Donated to the project. http://www.tngenweb.org/hardin. Sub-selection on *rootsweb* at *ancestry.com*. Years utilized: 1894 -1899.

Harris Chapel Holiness Church. "Old Brush Arbor Days." www.harrischapelholinesschurch.org/history.htm.

Hogan, Dorothy Hargrove. "Hargrove History."

Holden, Miriam Bell. "Memories, Memories – 1913 –." Quoted in Stokes, "The Bell Family at Shiloh."

Key, Melody. "The Pioneer Log Cabin: Productive Resources in Arkansas." *Bessie B. Moore Center for Economic Education.* http://bmcee.uark.edu/default.asp?target=teachingresources&show=lessons.

Lee, General Robert E. Quoted in *Tennessee and the Civil War.* http://www.tngenweb.org/civilwar.

Lee, Ronald F. *The Origin and Evolution of the National Military Park Idea.* 1973. National Park Service. http://www.nps.gov/history/history/online_books/history_military.

Lipson-Walker, Carolyn. "Weddings." In _*Encyclopedia of Southern Culture*_. Charles Reagan Wilson and William Ferris, eds. Chapel Hill: University of North Carolina Press, 1989. Sourced from Vicki Betts, Reference Librarian, University of Texas-Tyler.

---. "Childbirth" In _*Encyclopedia of Southern Culture*_. Charles Reagan Wilson and William Ferris, eds. Chapel Hill: University of North Carolina Press, 1989. Sourced from Vicki Betts, Reference Librarian, University of Texas-Tyler.

Logsdon, David R., ed. *Eyewitnesses at the Battle of Shiloh.* Nashville, TN: Kettle Mills Press, 1994.

Lossing, Benson J. *Pictorial History of the Civil War in the United States of America.* Hartford: T. Belknap, Publisher, 1868. Internet Archive. http://www.archive.org/details/pictorialhistory02loss.

McDonough, James Lee. *Shiloh – in Hell before Night.* Knoxville: The University of Tennessee Press, 1977.

Mehaffey, Karen Rae. "Mourning the Dead: Stages of Mourning for the Bereaved." *Citizen's Companion, The Voice of Civilian Reenacting.* Morristown, TN. www.citizenscompanion.com/news/view_sections.asp?id category=9&idarticle=378.

National Park Service. *Civil War Soldiers and Sailors System.* http://www.itd.nps.gov/cwss.

Newspaper interview of Mrs. A. V. Carothers, Sylvester, Fisher County, Texas, 1939.

Parson, Thomas E., Park Ranger. "Manse George Cabin, Preservation Project, Phase I, 2003." Shiloh National Military Park. Pittsburg Landing, TN.

Retreat and Vacation Homes in Sumner County, Tennessee. "Stay Down on the Farm." http://www.staydownonthefarm.com/around.php.

Sevier County Arkansas. "Lockesburg Cemetery." ARGENWEB. www.genealogyshoppe.com/arsevier/lockescem.htm.

Shedd, Charles E., Jr., Park Historian. "A History of Shiloh National Military Park Tennessee, 'The Coming of the White Man.'" *Park Administration and History, Shiloh National Military Park.* http://www.nps.gov/archive/shil/admhisint3.htm.

Shiloh National Military Park, Tennessee – Mississippi. "Park Administration and History, Land Protection Plan." 2002 Biennial Review. http://www.nps.gov/archive/shil/admlpp.htm.

Smith, Timothy B. *This Great Battlefield of Shiloh: History, Memory, and the Establishment of a Civil War National Military Park.* Knoxville: The University of Tennessee Press, 2004.

---. *The Untold Story of Shiloh: The Battle and the Battlefield.* Knoxville: The University of Tennessee Press, 2006.

Staff Writer. "The Civil War Comes to Hardin County, TN." *Savannah Courier.* http://www.hardinhistory.com/history/war.htm. (Currently invalid link).

Stansberry, Donna W. "Burial Practices in Southern Appalachia." Master of Arts in Liberal Studies thesis. Department of Cross Disciplinary Studies, East Tennessee State University, December 2004.
http://etd-submit.etsu.edu/etd/theses/available/etd-1112104-101034. Sourced from Vicki Betts, Reference Librarian, University of Texas-Tyler.

Stokes, Gaye Granger. "The Bell Family at Shiloh."

Strawn, Emmet Dee, compiler. *Strawn Genealogy.* Self-published, 1970.

Sword, Wiley. *Shiloh: Bloody April.* Dayton, OH: Morningside House, 2001.

Taylor, Joe Gray. *Eating, Drinking, and Visiting in the South: An Informal History.* Baton Rouge: Louisiana State University Press, 1982. Sourced from Vicki Betts, Reference Librarian, University of Texas-Tyler.

Tennessee Archeology Net. Hosted by Dr. Kevin E. Smith, Department of Sociology and Anthropology, Middle Tennessee State University. "Current Research in Tennessee Archaeology Annual Meeting Abstracts – 1994-2007." http://frank.mtsu.edu/~kesmith/TNARCH/CRITA/CRITA_Abstracts.html.

The Looking Glass, ed./comp., Hatfield, AR. *Lockesburg The First One Hundred 1878-1978.* Delight, AR: Alexander Printing, 1978.

War Department. *The War of the Rebellion: a Compilation of the Official Records of the Union and Confederate Armies*. Series 1 – Vol. 10 (Part I). Washington DC: GPO, 1884. Cornell University Library. http://cdl.library.cornell.edu/cgi-bin/moa/sgml/moa-idx?notisid=ANU4519-0010.

Weslager, C. A. *The Log Cabin in America: From Pioneer Days to the Present*. New Brunswick, N.J.: Rutgers University Press, 1969. McAlester, Virginia and Lee. *A Field Guide to American Houses*. New York: Alfred A. Knopf, 1984. Sourced from National Park Service. http://www.nps.gov/nr/twhp/wwwlps/lessons/4logcabins/4facts1.htm.

Wicker, Richard Fenton, Jr., ed. *The New Whicker/Wicker Family, Revised and Enlarged*. Virginia Beach, VA: Wicker Publishing, 1997.

Unrau, Harlan D. and G. Frank Williss. "Chapter Three: Impact of the New Deal on the National Park Service." *Administrative History: Expansion of the National Park Service in the 1930s*. September 1983. http://www.nps.gov/history/history/online_books/unrau-williss/adhi3c.htm.

Appendix #1:
Wicker Entry #1723

... passed the 2nd day of November 1847. 14th Range
of Section 3rd Beginning 10 poles North of the Southeast Corner of a 274
Acre Entry in the name of John Manley, Thence North 123 poles, Thence
East 40 poles, Thence South 76 poles, Thence West 14 poles, Thence South
47 poles, Thence West to the beginning. 5th Feby 1849

Manuel McClain ec

1723 State of Tennessee } Lewis Wicker assignee of Joseph Crownover
Hardin County } & Austin Halley Enters 400 Acres of land
in Accordance with an act of the General Assembly of said State passed
the 2nd of November 1847 on the waters of Snake Creek in Range 6 of Section
2 & 3 Beginning on the South west Corner of Entry No 1829 in the name of
Joseph Crownover, Thence East 217 poles, Thence North 88 poles, Thence
East 12 poles, North 236 poles, West 136 poles, South 72 poles, West 83
poles South 252 poles to the beginning 6 November 1848

Lewis Wicker ec

1724 State of Tennessee } The heirs of Thomas Collins Enter 150 Acres
Hardin County } of land in Accordance with an Act of the
General Assembly of said State passed the 2 day of November 1847
in Range 14th of Section 1 (Originally 8 District) Beginning
On the Northeast Corner of McDonalds 160 Acre Entry, Thence
South 150 poles to a white oak. Thence East 140 poles, Thence
North ...

Appendix #2: Definition Of Terms[136]

Warping board – a weaving tool.

Riven boards – having been split.

Auger – tool for boring holes.

Maul – wooden-headed hammer.

Clapboards – narrow board usually thicker at one edge than the other used for siding.

Whipsawed – whipsaw is a certain type of saw, several feet in length.

Hank – a coiled or looped bundle in weaving.

Quill – bobbin, spool, or spindle on which filling yarn is wound.

---

[136] *Dictionary and Thesaurus - Merriam-Webster Online*, http://www.merriam-webster.com/.

Appendix #3: Historical Base Map (Partial)

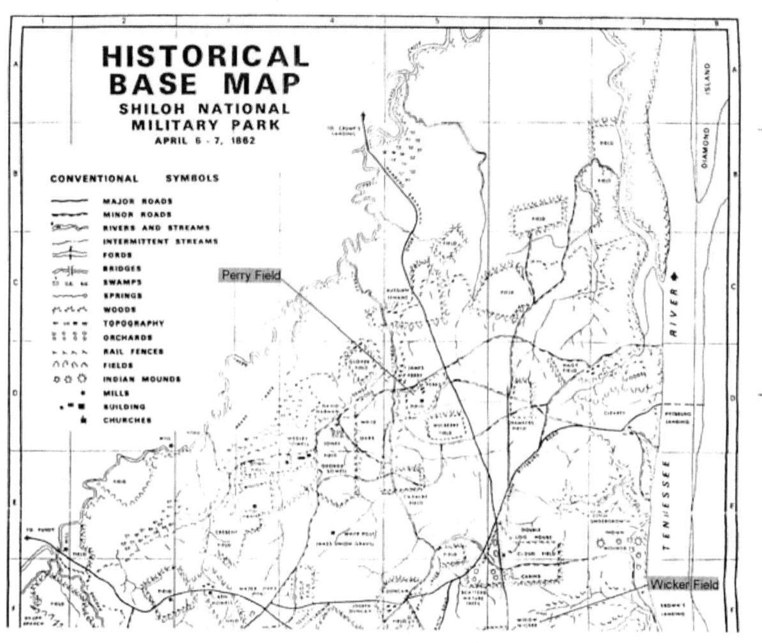

Appendix #4: Excavation Results - Courtesy Of Dr. Ellen Shlasko

CHAPTER 6

Excavation Results
Sarah Bell Farm Survey

June 2000

A team from the University of Memphis conducted archaeological testing of the Sarah Bell Farm site in June 2000. This survey area is found on the east side of the Hamburg-Savannah Road, directly opposite the Peach Orchard (Figure 6.1). The project had as its aim the location of two structures depicted on historic maps. The function and date of these buildings is unknown. The project design also included an opportunity to compare the value of metal detecting versus shovel testing as survey techniques. Finally, as previously mentioned, the farm owned by Sarah Bell was an important location during the battle of Shiloh. It was hoped that the metal detector survey would provide information about the distribution of bullets in the field, information that could be used to recreate troop movements during the battle.

Metal Detector Survey

During the metal detector survey of the Sarah Bell field, over 150 "hits" produced 154 recovered artifacts (Figure 6.2). These artifacts fall into three categories: military, domestic, and indeterminate.

Military artifacts

In 1909, Ambrose Bierce described the sights at Shiloh on the second day of battle:

Angular bits of iron, concavo-convex, sticking in the sides of muddy depressions, showed where shells had exploded in their furrows. Knapsacks, canteens, haversacks distended with soaken and swollen biscuits, gaping to disgorge, blankets beaten into the soil by the rain, rifles with bent barrels or splintered stocks, waist-belts, hats and the omnipresent sardine-box – all the wretched debris of the battle still littered the spongy earth as far as one could see, in every direction (Bierce 1909:10).

The soft ground absorbed these and other objects as soldiers passed and, later, as farmers returned to plow their fields.

Most of the military artifacts found during the metal detector survey were various forms of ammunition. Thirty-eight artifacts, representing nearly 25 percent of the total assemblage, were bullets, shot or fragments of artillery shell. Of these, 35 were bullets and musket balls of various calibers and designs.

The distribution of bullets and shot reflects the complex movement of battle through this area during the two days of fighting. The ammunition is spread around the perimeter of the field, as would be expected if troops avoided the open area for the cover provided by the surrounding brush. The distribution of bullets and shot also suggest that the structures located in the field were standing at the time of the battle. As can be seen in the accompanying figure (Figure 6.3), there is a gap in the distribution of bullets in the same location as the building foundation discovered during the testing of the site.

Other artifacts associated with the military occupation of the site reflect the personal lives of the soldiers. These include a Civil War era tent stake, lead poker chips, harmonica reeds, tent or raincoat grommets, and several gun parts and uniform accoutrements (Figure 6.4).

Domestic artifacts

Nails represent the largest class of domestic artifacts recovered in the survey. Thirty-nine of the metal detector hits were nails and nail fragments. With one exception, these nails were all cut or wrought nails, suggesting that they came from a structure built before the introduction of the wire nail in the mid-1850s. The absence of wire nails in the assemblage also suggests that the structures were no longer in use by the mid-1870s, when wire nails became common.

The distribution of nails differs from that of bullets and shot. Nails are concentrated in a smaller area of the site, in the south half of the field and along the west edge (Figure 6.5).

Miscellaneous artifacts

It is impossible to determine a precise origin for a number of artifacts. Separating military from domestic artifacts, as discussed previously, can be difficult. For instance, the survey turned up a number of horseshoes and other pieces of horse furniture. These objects might be related to battle events – after all, the Union battery that held this location on the morning of April 6th is known to have lost a large number of horses prior to abandoning this position; horses that would have been burnt in place or nearby in the days following the battle. However, it is equally possible that these objects are remains from the farming operations on the site.

Other objects in the miscellaneous category include various tools and agricultural implements, including a file, a wrench, and tractor or plow parts.

Artifact Distribution

The metal detector survey revealed a pattern of artifact distribution around the survey area that deviates from a random distribution. The bulk of the objects were located in an arc that runs from the northwest corner of the field, down the west side of the field and across the south end of the field, gradually tapering off towards the east edge of the survey area. The northeast quadrant of the survey area is virtually devoid of artifacts. This is not a function of differential survey practices, as the entire area was systematically covered during a single day of survey by the same teams using the same equipment.

Object Term	Number	Percentage of total
Ammunition	35	23.0
Belly band	1	.5
Bit	1	.5
Bolt	4	2.5
Bottle	1	.5
Bridle	5	3.5
Buckle	1	.5
Button	1	.5
Butt plate	2	1.5
Canister	1	.5
Poker chip	4	2.5
Clock	1	.5
Cup	1	.5

Object Term	Number	Percentage of total
Dish	1	.5
File	1	.5
Grommet	2	1.5
Harmonica	2	1.5
Hinge	2	1.5
Horseshoe	3	2.0
Jar	2	1.5
Knife	1	.5
Metal Fragments	28	18.0
Nail	39	25.5
Nut	2	1.5
Ring	1	.5
Artillery shell	2	1.5
Strap	1	.5
Stud	1	.5
Teapot	1	.5
Tent stake	1	.5
Tractor piece	2	1.5
Washer	2	1.5
Wire fragment	1	.5
Wrench	1	.5
TOTAL	154	99.5*

Table 6.1 - Artifacts from Metal Detector Survey

Shovel Test Survey

The excavation team dug a total of twenty shovel tests, only nine of which were positive. Of these positive tests, only three contained more than one artifact. The positive tests were clustered in the center of the survey area. This was in striking contrast to the metal detector survey, which located objects throughout the survey area.

* Due to rounding error this number does not equal 100 percent.

One shovel test did contain a number of artifacts. This test (FS199), located at 120N 150E, yielded a large amount of conglomerate, a locally available building material widely used for constructing foundations. Enlarging the test to 30 x 50 cm. allowed the excavator to see sizeable pieces of conglomerate, apparently *in situ*. The enlarged test also contained a variety of artifacts, including nails, glass and ceramic.

Object term	Number	Percent of total
Glass containers	6	21.5
Brick	1	4.0
Lithic flakes	2	7.0
Metal fragments	2	7.0
Nails	12	43.0
Ceramic fragments	5	18.0
Total	28	100.5*

Table 6.2 - Artifacts from Shovel Test Survey

Test Unit Excavation

Upon encountering the rubble foundation in shovel test 120N 150E, the team decided to excavate a 2 x 2 meter test unit in order to determine the size and preservation of the feature. The plow zone, consisting of 10 centimeters of homogenous dark brown loam, was removed from the unit, allowing the excavation team to clearly define the southeast corner of an intact building foundation. The foundation consisted of large chunks of naturally occurring conglomerate, bound together with mortar (Figure 6.6). The use of conglomerate for the foundation does not provide much evidence about the structure's function, as this was a common building material throughout the area, used for buildings of all kinds. The foundation was approximately 40 centimeters thick. Excavation of the test unit exposed 1.7 meters of the south wall and 1.2 meters of the east wall. Outside the foundation wall, on the south and east sides of the test unit, was a light yellowish-brown, sterile, sandy-clay subsoil. The interior fill consisted of an artifact rich, grayish-brown organic layer of unknown depth.

Because the goal of the research was simply to locate remains, rather than to excavate them, there was no attempt to excavate the feature fill.

Artifacts from Unit 1

The excavation of Unit 1 yielded only fifteen artifacts, including four ceramic shards, nine glass fragments, a piece of mortar and an iron button ring. The original shovel test that located the foundation contained an additional thirteen artifacts, including four more pieces of ceramic, five bottle glass fragments, two nails, an unidentified iron object and a stone flake.

The ceramics from this unit consist of typical mid to late nineteenth century ceramics. These include an ironstone saucer, two pieces of whiteware, and two fragments of stoneware.

Object Term	Number	Percentage of Total
Glass fragments	9	60.0
Ceramic fragments	4	26.5
Brick	1	6.5
Button	1	6.5
Total	15	99.5*

Table 5.3 - Artifacts from Excavation Unit

Summary

The survey at the Sarah Bell Farm was successful in satisfying its primary goal: pinpointing the location of one of the structures seen on the historic maps. The building foundations found in the excavation unit are the type of simple conglomerate and mortar foundation expected in a farm outbuilding or tenant structure. However, because the fill was not excavated it is impossible to determine the use of the building.

The second goal, to compare the use of metal detector survey and shovel test survey, produced extremely interesting results. The survey of the Sarah Bell Farm clearly showed that on nineteenth century sites like Shiloh the metal detectors more accurately identified the presence of subsurface remains. If the survey had relied on shovel testing alone, it is unlikely that the survey team would have located the structure. The high concentration of nails found during the metal detector phase of the testing determined the placement of shovel tests and encouraged the survey team to excavate the additional tests that eventually led to the discovery of the building. These results are similar to comparisons of survey techniques that have been conducted on Civil War sites (Sterling and Slaughter 2000). However, although metal detecting provides an excellent view of the distribution of artifacts on a site, the actual foundations were found through the excavation of shovel tests.

Index

Duane Helweg

Duane was born in San Angelo, Texas to a German father, Otto Helweg, and a Scotch-Irish mother, Wanda Montgomery. He survived polio and a tornado there before growing up to attend Angelo State and Texas Tech before graduating from Arizona State University. He spent a career working for the State of Arizona buying freeways. Duane helped raise a girl Kara and a boy Carl and retired back to San Angelo where he met and now lives with wife, Sharon.

He has written family histories for both sides of his parent's families. His articles and stories have been printed in genealogical journals (*The Chisholm Trail*), newspapers (*New Ulm Enterprise*) and newsletters (*Texas German Society Reporter*). One editor says he can take dry facts and dates and weave them into histories that make his ancestors "come alive." Duane has spoken at or done readings to church and historical groups. He also has spoken, and still speaks, to Lions Clubs in Texas about his experiences as both a camper and counselor at their summer camp for disabled children.

His Tennessee history is from his mother's families. Names like: Wicker, Buchanan, Hooker, Reed, Anderson, Lipford, Witt, Montgomery, Russell and Patterson, form ancestry in the counties Hardin, McNairy, Hamilton and Rhea. Duane's son is a banker and daughter a teacher and both received degrees and live in Tennessee.

The author may be emailed at: info@rimrockwritings.com

What others are saying about the book...

"Certain phrases of alliteration astound us, and give us a good feeling of a profound contribution you have made to the literary world of a lone cabin in Tennessee."
– Howard & Margaret Montgomery, University of Texas Alumni

"For Civil War buffs, this will shed new light on 'bloody Shiloh,' one of the most horrific battles fought between the Union and Confederate armies. Although a technical victory for northern forces, it was overshadowed by appalling losses, costing 13,000 Union casualties and nearly 11,000 Confederates. Duane Helweg has done a remarkable job telling the personal story of one family in the midst of this tragic war."
– Ross McSwain, retired award winning journalist and author of eight books...has worked with Helweg through the *San Angelo Writers Club* in Texas.

"...your manuscript, Lone Survivor at Shiloh ....is business-like and professional. You have a lot of very good folklore in it, the kind of how-they-did-it information we don't often find about practices and methods of the past. For instance, the ash hopper, preparing for funerals, etc..."
– Elmer Kelton, Voted *Best Western Author of All-Time*, Several-Time *Spur Award* and *Western Heritage Award* Winner.